Rave Reviews

"This book is a 'must read' at our company. It gives our sales team that added edge in a competitive sales environment; I recommend you keep this book on your desk or on your coffee table. It is only fair to give people a warning you can practically read their mind."

– Blaire Fanning,
CEO MCAads / Russell Johns Associates

....

"It's so interesting that I couldn't put it down and I learned plenty of new, useful information, especially about shaking hands. The illustrations are spot-on - accurate and hilarious. Everyone can benefit from reading this."

– Dr. Roberta Temes,
Psychotherapist and Author

....

"Michael C. Anthony is Dr. Body Language! I use the techniques I learned from him whenever I present to an audience and get fantastic results!"

– Dr. Mike Mandel, NLP Trainer

....

"This book is pure gold for anyone that wants to understand the true secrets of body language and master the art of non-verbal communication."

– Mikey Nagle, Author, Speaker, Trainer

....

"As a Mystifier, my job is to make the audience believe the impossible. Body Language is a huge part of that. This book will help you communicate on a whole new level."

– Mike Super, Winner of NBC's Phenomenon and America's Got Talent Finalist

....

"As witty as it is practical, Michael C. Anthony's Body Language Secrets offers us a fun, simple way of improving how we communicate. Go buy his book, it will change the way you see the world, and how the world sees you!"

– Lisa Dadd, Speaker, Author

BODY LANGUAGE SECRETS

How to Read Minds by reading bodies

Michael C. Anthony

BODY LANGUAGE SECRETS:
How to Read Minds by Reading Bodies

Visit www.michaelcanthony.com

ISBN: 978-1499159554

PUBLISHER
Osurac Publishing, 2014
Tampa, FL

Printed in the United States of America

COVER DESIGN: Osurac Design
ILLUSTRATIONS: Phil Juliano www.bestinshowcomic.com
FRONT COVER PHOTOGRAPHY: Lilly Caruso
FOREVER GRATEFUL: To my brother Joe.
Thanks for the kidney!

For speaking, training, media appearances or
bulk quantities of this book, contact us at
www.michaelcanthony.com

NOTE TO YOU THE READER

Table of Contents

HELLO THERE!

Wordless Wisdom

I speak two languages, Body and English.

—Mae West

How long does it take for another person to get that "first" impression of you? A minute? 30 seconds?

Guess again. In just 10 to 15 seconds, someone grabs an almost-instant impression and sizes you up accordingly and you don't have to say a word. Your body is doing all the talking. Do you know what your eyes, posture, hands, and face are revealing? When you think you're showing a confident, attentive, or interested demeanor, your body may be telling a different story.

Body language is the all-important, silent communication that surrounds us everyday—at work or home, in the mall, at the airport, and in your favorite restaurant. People can't help but give off their true feelings, thoughts, or intentions through their body language, often involuntarily and unknowingly. It's in the eyes, the mouth, the shoulders, the arms, the hands, the legs, the feet, the breathing, and the gestures. The space you create between yourself and other people sends a message. The way you handle inanimate objects, like a pen, glasses, coffee mug, cigarette, or clothing offers clues to what you're thinking. It's unavoidable.

How many times have you met someone in any situation - business, social orotherwise—and thought, "Wow, I like this guy. He has it all together", or on the contrary, "Wow, this person rubs me the wrong way. I don't think I can trust her"?

Where do these feelings come from? Are we clairvoyant or is it just a vibe? Is it intuition or genius instinct? Do we have a sixth sense or are we really capable of knowing somebody else's thoughts, motives, and opinions just by looking at them?

The answer is... well... all of the above. It just depends on how we want to view our amazing hidden gift. Understanding body language comes from our instincts initially. But when we get into the fun details and grasp the "whats", "whys", and "hows" of non-verbal communication, we will be able to pick up "tells" that would make David Copperfield proud.

Sometimes, these fast assessments hit like a "gut feeling"— raising the hair on the back of your neck, activating an anxious feeling in your stomach, making you draw back or move in closer. In reality, you're subconsciously getting a read from that person's body language. Your brain is receiving visual signals that you may not even be aware of.

EVERY BODY POSITION—SUBTLE OR OBVIOUS—HAS A "NOT-SO-HIDDEN" MEANING.

I've been studying and teaching body language for more than 15 years. I train corporations, executives, and sales teams to become masters of non-verbal communication. They discover not only what to look for in the body language of others, but how to use their own bodies to negotiate, persuade, and sell to others.

Often organizations hire me in to train them in an entertaining, educational way—enter-training, if you will. I take on the role of a mind-reader and proceed to do what looks like the impossible. I tell people what number they are thinking of, I persuade them to make decisions I have previously predicted, and I become a human polygraph machine while executives see if they can get a lie past me. They can't.

To perform these apparent miracles, I use a plethora of techniques I've mastered over the years and one of those techniques is the art and science of reading body language.

After you read this little gem you are currently holding, you too will have the ability to see things in a whole new and very obvious way. Picking up on somebody else's true emotions won't just be a psychological hunch anymore; you'll have the cold, hard specifics to back up your hunches and turn them into cold, hard facts, You'll spot dishonesty, you'll be aware of feigned interest, you'll spot hidden contempt, subtle nervousness, and hidden aggression. You'll know how to use your body to build rapport with that new client or prospect. You'll learn what to look for in a job interview, regardless of which side of the table you are sitting on. You'll learn how to use your body during that all-important presentation, so you come across as clear, concise, and confident. You'll learn what's behind that poker face across the table when you are negotiating an important deal. You'll even know what your "special someone" might really be thinking.

STEEPLING – THIS HAND POSITION SHOWS
CONFIDENCE AND EXPERTISE.

You'll also learn to alter your handshake so it will communicate exactly the message you want to send. Many people fail to understand the importance of a handshake. Love 'em or hate 'em, the ritual is here to stay, and being a master hand-shaker is a vital skill.

And perhaps most importantly, you'll learn how to control your own body language in order to project the impression you want.

It doesn't matter whether you are trying to influence a customer, impress the boss, manipulate the person on the other side of the negotiation table, or detect dishonesty in a co-worker, employee, vendor, or other person in your world. The time you invest in learning non-verbal, body language delivers an exceptional return.

MICHAEL'S TIP

Be careful! People will size you up in less than 15 seconds—often, before you've even said a word.

I've written this book to show you the "who", "what", "where", "when", "why", and "how" of body language, so you can unleash the power for yourself. I'm going to make it fun and at the same time, give you new strategies that will serve you for a lifetime. This book takes you into belly of the beast. By the end of the book—and with some practice—you'll be so fluent that you will be able to read people like a book. All this knowledge equips you with an arsenal of tools that will be with you at all times, so you can apply them on your unsuspecting clients, colleagues, bosses, and friends. You'll have the unfair advantage to not only give your best impression, but you'll learn how to effectively "Read Minds by Reading Bodies".

Like learning any language, proficiency takes some practice. I encourage you to take what you are learning and put it into practice. Go out and view it in real-world, people watching expeditions. The next time you go the airport, the grocery store, a business meeting, or your mother-in-law's house, watch people like an old-time silent movie, and you'll be amazed how you can write your own subtitles that coincide to what you are seeing.

Ready? Let's dive in!

Michael

Body Talk and Business

> The time to stop talking is when the other person nods his head affirmatively, but says nothing.
>
> —Helen Keller

So how important is body language? To understand its value, we need to look at communication as a whole. A person who is on the receiving end of our communication is being bombarded with far more than just words, so let's break it down.

Communication Breakdown

Words: These are the actual words that come out of our mouth. Nouns, pronouns, verbs etc. We often think that our words are the most important element of getting our point across. Are they? We'll soon find out.

Vocal: Tone, speed, volume, and pitch. There are the actual sounds and pacing of those words just mentioned. Vocals play an important role... but how important?

Body Language: The non-verbals include the eyes, mouth, arms, shoulders, hands, legs, feet, sitting, standing, and so much more. Important? Oh yes.

Behavioral scientists have researched these three forms of communication and discovered just how important each of them are to the other person/people receiving your communication. Here's what they discovered.

Our Words: 7%: Yes, words comprise only 7% of our communication. Remember that next time you are creating a presentation or a speech and plan to deliver it, word for word. Words alone aren't nearly as important as we may have thought.

Tone: 37%: That's a big jump when compared to words. This statistic means that others consider your tone of voice, volume, and the speed at which yours words come out of your mouth to be far more important than the words themselves.

Body Language 55%: Whoa, slow down. 55%? It's quite astonishing that our silent communication is perceived as far more important than what is coming out of our mouths. The way we physically hold ourselves is the undisputed champion of communication. Just think of the advantage you are going to have when you learn the all-important skill set we call body language!

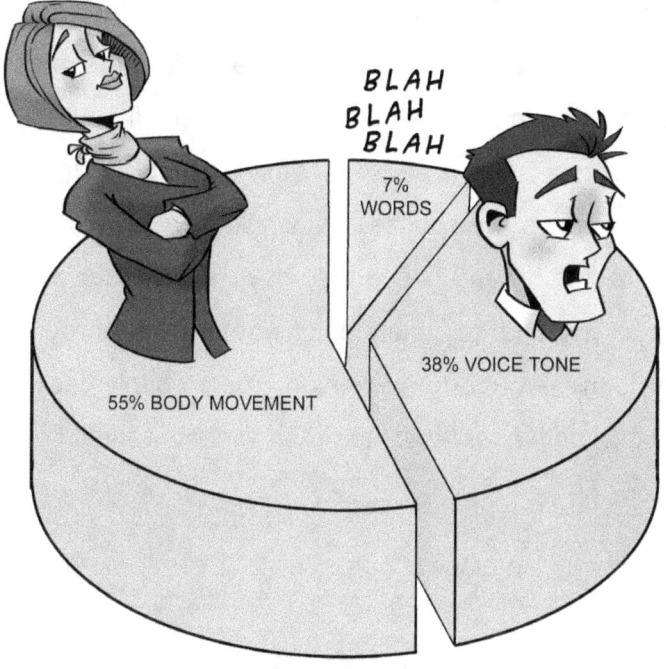

BLAH
BLAH
BLAH

7%
WORDS

38% VOICE TONE

55% BODY MOVEMENT

BODY MOVEMENT – THE UNDISPUTED CHAMPION

Body language—non-verbal expressions—clearly speak louder than words. From the movement of your eyes to the way you sit, stand, shake a hand, smile, twitch, nod, fold your arms or legs, tap your fingers, or any motion, you send messages to the people around you. And, most of the time, you don't even realize it.

Body language is not as complex as some forms of communication. You don't have to conjugate a verb or concern yourself with dangling participles. But you should be aware of what your non-verbal cues are telling others, and vice versa, so that you don't miss valuable messages.

Body language is the management of space, appearance, posture, gesture, voice, eye contact, facial expression breathing, touch, and smell. Don't think smell matters? Oh yes, it does. Smell is sensed by the amygdala in the brain, which triggers a response, like wrinkling your nose. If you meet a person and notice they have a bad odor because of poor hygiene, too many onions at lunch or an overdose of cologne—you form an opinion. You probably back away and this motion tells that individual, "I don't want to be close to you."

That's body language.

GUESS WHO'S BODY LANGUAGE IS SAYING,
"DISGUSTED".

> **ki•ne•sics**—*n*. the study of body movements, gestures, facial expressions, etc., as a systematic mode of communication

A Little History

Where did the study of body language begin? Strangely enough, it can actually be pin-pointed to a specific time and place. The year was 1960. Vice President Nixon and John F. Kennedy were in the first televised presidential debate.

In 1960 only about half of the American households owned a television which made the opinions after the debate even more interesting, as you are about to find out.

Kennedy was advised to wear make-up, as was Nixon. Kennedy wore make-up and looked healthy and vibrant, yet Nixon refused to wear make-up as it seemed unnatural. As it turned out, many viewers thought Nixon looked older and unhealthy. At this point the advantage goes to Kennedy.

During the debate both men were very well spoken. Kennedy held excellent posture and poise while Nixon's demeanor seemed a little less convincing. Nixon leaned on the podium and his eyes wandered—especially when Kennedy was speaking, as he didn't think the cameras were focused on him. Nixon even wiped perspiration from his face with a handkerchief. It may have been due to the heat from the studio lights, but visually, he appeared anxious.

When Americans were polled after the debate some interesting facts came in. Those who watched the debate on television thought that Kennedy won the debate by a large margin, yet those who listened to the debate on the radio chose Nixon as the front-runner. The victory ended up going to Kennedy.

What does this say about watching a person, as opposed to simply listening to their words? It means the body says much more than words alone. In fact, the visuals mean more than the words. End of debate.

Unspoken "Uh Oh" Moments

You're sitting in an interview and the prospective employer asks you the reason you're leaving your current employer. You pause. Your eyes move upward and look to the right. The interviewer, who is knowledgeable in body language, nods and makes a note. She then asks you why you want to join this company. You fold your arms in front of you and make the same eye movement.

You leave the interview thinking you nailed it.

But you didn't. The interviewer understood your body language and determined you were being dishonest.

In another situation, you're at a business mixer, speaking with a potential client. You're being wonderfully conversational and witty. "Great," you think to yourself, "this guy is loving me!"

If you had looked down, you would have seen that his feet were pointed slightly away from you, towards another group of people. His body language, had you noticed it, would have told you that he didn't want to be standing there with you, but was mentally directing himself to the other group.

You're in a negotiation meeting, trying to firm up a deal with a businessman from Japan. He hands you his business card. You take it with your left hand, make a quick note on the back, and staple it to a folder. The businessman frowns slightly, which you don't notice. He excuses himself from the meeting. You have just offended him and the chance of closing this deal—at least, today—has become far less likely.

SHE'S TALKING, BUT DOES HE LOOK INTERESTED?

Clueless is Careless

Our own bodies could be betraying us! And I don't mean the extra weight it won't discard, the dwindling memory, or the hair that has a mind of its own. I'm talking about the involuntary responses—our body language vocabulary.

Think about these simple movements or postures:

- ✓ Stand with your hands in your pockets
- ✓ Nod quickly when someone is speaking
- ✓ Run your hands through your hair
- ✓ Shake your leg or foot when you're sitting down
- ✓ Bite your lip
- ✓ Slouch
- ✓ Tap your pen on the table
- ✓ Glance at your watch
- ✓ Scratch your neck
- ✓ Cross your arms when speaking to someone
- ✓ Pick your nose
- ✓ Tug your ear
- ✓ Point to the group you're presenting to

✓ Hold a drink in front of you with both hands

✓ Fold your arms across your chest with your hands under your armpits

✓ Touch your mouth or nose while speaking

Everything on this list sends a negative signal. You're non-verbally communicating that you're nervous, bored, unconfident, distrusting, or possibly lying,

Do you do any of these things? More importantly, do you even *know* if and when you do? Your body may be betraying you. So let's get a handle on these non-verbal cues that follow and take control of our communication.

As you work through this book, you'll learn the meaning of a wide variety of movements and positions—positive and negative.

Every single day, people in business make non-verbal missteps that hinder their success. They unknowingly give negative signals that are picked up by other people— consciously or subconsciously. By controlling your body language, you can communicate the messages you want— honesty, confidence, interest, attraction—and even mask the ones you'd rather conceal—boredom, distrust, disinterest, and annoyance to name just a few.

Careers That Require Body Language Fluency

Here's just a sample of professionals who have to rely on controlling their body language and understanding it in others:

Actors and actresses

Animal trainers

Athletes

Auctioneers

Bullfighters

Coaches

Consultants

Entertainers

Healthcare providers

Human resource professionals

Lawyers

Managers

Mimes

Military

Service people

Negotiators

News reporters

Poker players

Police officers

Recruiters

Referees and Umpires

Salespeople

Speakers and Presenters

Teachers

Therapists

Wait staff

You know what? It's actually easier to specify occupations that don't require body language skills. If you have a job where you never see another person, then you are exempt—as far as your job goes. But what about the other areas of your life when you do see people? Gotcha! If you interact with others face-to-face, then your body language is in play.

Hermits... you are off the hook. Everybody else... be on guard.

IS BODY LANGUAGE IMPORTANT TO YOUR JOB?
IT MAY BE MORE IMPORTANT THAN YOU THINK!

Life is a Sales Job

Even if you don't make a career of selling, every job you have will require you to sell. Just getting the job demands that you sell yourself to the interviewer. When you have a great idea—well, that's great in your eyes—you then have to sell it to someone else, like your boss or an investor.

A few years ago, I was contacted to do a screen test for a TV show. I have a history of helping people rid themselves of nasty, lifelong fears and this TV program was essentially going to showcase people with phobias. Then, I would come in and save the day by talking them out of their fear by using some mental and verbal gymnastics.

The screen test was scheduled to take place in Los Angeles at the office of famed reality TV producer Mark Burnett. (Survivor, The Apprentice, Shark Tank, The Voice) It was essentially an interview with me in front of the camera, curing a woman of her fear of mice. The producers wanted to see how I appeared and acted on camera.

Body language played an important role here. Of course, this was about much more than my words, it was about how I was perceived as a whole.

I pulled out all the stops. I paid close attention to my posture. I smiled, held my chin up, and made the correct amount of eye contact. I kept an open position and gestured with my palms showing. I showed as much confidence as I could muster through my body. Did I get the job? Yes, I did. I later found out there were more than 20 people hoping to get the spot.

We shot the episode and everything went great. I cured a man of his fear of mannequins and cured a woman from her fear of bananas... yes, bananas.

MICHAEL'S TIP

The most important part of your communication doesn't make a sound.

Life is all about buying and selling, which is why understanding body language is so important. Whether you're trying to strike a deal on a new car or talk your way out of a ticket with a police officer, you're negotiating. When you're buying a car, selling a house, attempting to impress a date, client, boss, or dealing with your kids, you will give yourself a huge advantage when you can understand their non-verbal cues and send back the messages you want to deliver—maybe not so loud, but ever so clear!

Now let's go back to that "Don't" list and see what those cues are saying.

Stand with your hands in your pockets	Disinterested or possibly hiding something
Nod quickly when someone is speaking	Impatient
Run your hands through your hair	Exasperated, possibly flirtatious (female)
Shake your leg or foot when you're sitting down	Anxious, bored, possibly tired.

ANXIOUS? BORED? TIRED?

Holding the Chair & Shaking the foot	Anxious
Bite your lip	Tense
Slouch	Unconfident or bored
Tap your pen on the table	Nervous or bored
Glance at your watch	Bored
Scratch your neck	Doubt, possible dishonesty
Cross your arms when speaking to someone	Defensive
Pick your nose	Inattentive, stressed
Tug your ear	Indecisive
Point to the group you're presenting to drive home a powerful point	Perhaps exaggerating or lying

BEWARE OF THE FINGER POINT:
DRIVING HOME A POINT? OR LYING?

Hold a drink in front of you with both hands	Nervous, keeping hands busy
Fold your arms across your chest with your hands under your armpits	This could mean authoritative, nervous, insecure this person may simply be chilly.
Touch your mouth or nose while speaking	Lying or exaggerating

Let's Be REAL

As you examine the examples above and in other areas of this book, it's important to be real and to understand that not every gesture always has a psychological meaning. Sometimes a person gestures simply because it's what appears comfortable. So let's draw our line in the sand and have a basic understanding of what may be a real psychological gesture and what may simply be a body movement.

For example, when somebody crosses their arms across their chest, how can it mean both authoritative and insecure? It's important for us to be reasonable and look at the facts first. Is this person in a position of authority? Do they show other signs of confidence? Or is this person in a situation where they may be showing some insecurity? If so, it's time to keep looking for more clues of insecurity. What if it's chilly in the room and our arm-crosser is simply cold? Maybe he/she is leaning back in a chair with crossed arms because they are comfortable.

If somebody touches their mouth or nose while talking, is it a hard fact that they are lying or exaggerating? No. They may have an itch. Maybe they are checking for bread pudding on their lips.

In becoming a non-verbal sleuth, we need to look for congruence in those people we are studying. Don't be too quick to judge. Feel out the situation and look for repeat offenders. Judging too quickly can get you in trouble.

Language Lab

Here's where you start practicing your body language skills.

1. Look for instances where someone uses one of the non-verbal cues listed in this chapter. How did you react now that you consciously understand the message?

2. Purposely use some of the gestures listed under the Clueless is Careless section (a few pages back) during a conversation with someone you know. Notice their reaction. Do they move away? Seem irritated? Question you?

The Spongy Handshake and Other Greeting Gaffes

I can feel the twinkle of his eye in his handshake.

—Helen Keller

If you've ever shaken hands with someone and felt like you were either rubbing against a wet rag or being locked in a vice grip, you know that the gesture often prompts a visceral reaction—from pleasure to repulsion.

The handshake can say, "Hey, how you doin?" or seal a deal, although, nowadays, contracts and lawyers are involved because the good, ole handshake just doesn't have the credibility it once did.

But handshakes are still very important in the business world. Researchers tell us that handshakes can help us reach into a person's psyche and clue into their thoughts and intentions. The handshake will affirm if a person is a power player or sincere, if they are nervous, or overbearing, if they are hoping to belittle you, or desire to serve you. With so much on the line, it's essential to get a grip on this part of your body language vocabulary.

Whether giving or receiving, a handshake represents a powerful communication tool. In the business world, certainly, giving the wrong type of handshake can mean you've got some extra work to do to overcome a bad first impression. Remember the 55 percent non-verbal statistic? More than half of what you initially communicate to another person occurs without any words at all.

Greg Stewart, associate professor of management and organizations at the University of Iowa, led a study of the relationship of handshakes with job interview success. He said the handshake sets the tone for the rest of the interview.

"Job seekers are trained how to act in a job interview, how to talk, how to dress, how to answer questions, so we all look and act alike to varying degrees because we've all been told the same things," said Stewart. "But the handshake is something that's perhaps more individual and subtle, so it may communicate something that dress or physical appearance doesn't."

With something as personal as a handshake, think about the impact! So, let's get shaking and see what we can learn from this gesture.

A gripping history...

Why do we even shake hands when meeting someone? Think about it. Why not just wave, nod your head, or even bow like certain Asian cultures? Why the body contact? Well, the ritual has been traced back to ancient Greece. Around 5th century B.C., soldiers extended an open hand as a gesture to show that they were not carrying any weapons. Rather than shake hands, they grabbed one another's forearms instead.

The Dominator

As one of the most prevalent handshakes in the business world, the Dominator starts off as "normal", but then, the person who assumes he's dominant turns his wrist so his palm is facing downward and forces your palm to face upward. This shake can be considered quite rude by many people, but is accepted in some circumstances.

Donald Trump, proven Dominator, is likely to use this handshake with his colleagues—like claiming the power position. Most people would happily accept the opportunity to shake "The Donald's" hand and would overlook his need for palm power.

THE DOMINATOR

The employee may offer the submissive side of this handshake to his boss by turning his hand upward. This tells the boss, "I am here to serve." He is subtly giving authority to his employer.

Pay attention to the use of the Dominator. When someone uses it on you, think of what they are trying to communicate. Should you allow them to literally take the upper hand? Or should you make an effort to either shift the power or move to a neutral shake?

Heart in your hand

A firm handshake can mean more than confidence. It could be a telltale sign of your cardiovascular health! According to a decade-long study of about 2,500 men and women, people over 65 with a strong grip had a 42 percent lower risk of stroke. "Vascular problems in the brain manifest themselves in a wide variety of ways," explained study author Erica Camargo, MD, of the Boston Medical Center.

Source: Prevention.com

The Knuckle Buster

This one isn't a shake as much as it is a death grip. The force with which the Knuckle Buster is delivered has the potential to cause pain. At the very least, it's uncomfortable.

The giver of this handshake is attempting to intimidate the "handshakee", exerting considerable strength in the clench to show that they have more power than you, which may or may not be true.

THE KNUCKLE BUSTER

When I teach these handshake techniques to organizations, the Knuckle Buster always receives a shout of "YES!" from the audience. It seems everybody has been at the mercy of a knuckle-busting handshake. If you haven't, you are probably the one giving them. Gotcha!

There's a scene in the movie, "Predator" where Arnold Schwarzenegger and Carl Weathers ("Apollo Creed" in the first "Rocky" movie) play two Special Forces agents who are meeting again after a long time. They shake hands and the camera zooms in on their bulging biceps. The handshake is more like a clash of the titans as the two powerhouses attempt to establish their power position as the guy in charge.

You might also receive the Knuckle Buster handshake from a big guy who just doesn't know his own strength. After you are finished screaming, please tell the big oaf that he is hurting people with his handshake. He will either appreciate your advice because he didn't mean to squeeze so hard, or he will think you're overreacting. His response will tell you a lot about his character.

Note to men: Never try the Knuckle Buster on the ladies. First of all, you may actually crack a smaller knuckle. Secondly, you'll never fool the ladies with your false sense of power. They are usually smarter than us and not impressed by this show of misplaced strength.

Note to men: Never try the Knuckle Buster on the ladies. First of all, you may actually crack a smaller knuckle. Secondly, you'll never fool the ladies with your false sense of power.

They are usually smarter than us and not impressed by this show of misplaced strength.

Have you ever been on the receiving end of a Knuckle Buster? Do you recall what you thought of that person at the time? What was the non-verbal message you received?

The Sweaty Palm

All together now: "Ewwwww!"

The sweaty palm is probably the least desirable handshake—and you never see it coming. Suddenly, you're connecting with a sweaty, slippery palm that makes you cringe, recoil, and want to run to the restroom to rid yourself of a potential case of the swine flu.

Now, a sweat-soaked palm certainly isn't intentional, like the Dominator or Knuckle Buster. It's a physical sign that likely means the person is nervous—possibly about meeting you, a pending sales presentation, or just a chronically nervous individual.

THE SWEATY PALM

You might have an advantage here, because you're getting a quick insight into this individuals state. If this person is about to make a presentation to you, he or she is obviously uncertain and anxious for some reason. You can leverage that nervousness to get to the reason for the angst, which could be that he isn't convinced of his own sales pitch, or maybe he is inexperienced. If you're interviewing the Sweaty Palmer for a job, you might choose to put the person at ease.

Can you recall the last time you latched onto a sweaty palm? How did you react? Did you pull back and wipe the unpleasant moisture on your pant leg, a tissue, or some other absorbent surface? Did you automatically recognize this handshake as a sign of nervousness? Did you use this knowledge to your benefit?

> **You've got to hand it to them!**
>
> **World's longest handshake**: 42 hours and 35 minutes, achieved March 4-6, 2011, by Nepalese brothers, Dinesh and Pawan Timilsina, students at the Everest College of Multiple Studies in Kathmandu.
>
> **Most simultaneous handshakes at one event**: 24,435 Leuva Patel couples on January 23, 2012.
>
> **Most handshakes by a politician in one 8-hour period**: Gubernatorial candidate Bill Richardson shook hands with 13,392 people at the New Mexico State Fair and a tailgate party in Albuquerque— all without the use of hand sanitizer, because he said, "I've been offered it, but I've turned it down. I'm not afraid to get my hands dirty." But he did accept a bucket of ice for his sore hand.

The Brush Off

We all know what it's like to get dismissed by someone. Sometimes, it's blatantly clear, while on other occasions, the message is subtle. When it comes to handshakes, the Brush Off is easy to recognize.

This handshake happens when the shaker is in a hurry, doesn't care or would rather be somewhere else. They shake your hand and get it over with so quickly that you aren't even sure it happened. There's barely a connection—like "air kisses" and with the same lack of sincerity. The giver might want to get it over with because the handshake seems unnecessary or unimportant.

THE BRUSH OFF

The quick handshake is usually accompanied by a lack of eye contact, another signal of disinterest or distraction. The Brush Off hand shaker is on the lookout for someone he feels is more important than you—or as important as he thinks he is. Look at the person's feet when you're receiving this handshake. The toes are pointing in the direction of his interest. Are his feet pointing toward you? If not, it's a sure sign that the handshake is meaningless—at least, to him.

The world is full of these individuals who may be stepping on people on their way up the ladder. Don't worry though—you can wave goodbye when he's on his way down too.

When have you encountered a Brush Off handshake? What was your reaction? Did you get the message? Conversely, can you remember being the one to deliver this dismissive gesture? Was it intentional?

The Controller

This aggressive shaker grabs your hand enthusiastically and pulls you off balance while moving your hand in every direction except the one you are ready for. This handshake could reflect an overly exuberant personality, but is often used by a person who wants to dominate this situation. They are like puppeteers, pulling your strings with a yank of your hand. The Controller is trying to convey that they are large and in charge—which they usually aren't. They are basically saying, "Hey, I'm lacking everywhere else but check out this handshake." Woo hoo—enjoy the ride.

THE CONTROLLER

There are some similarities between the Controller and the Knuckle Buster. Both are dominating. Sometimes the giver of these handshakes is a person who doesn't realize his own strength and is putting you on their "Tilt O' Whirl" without even realizing it. These people should at least give you a vomit bag with their free hand.

Just as with the Knuckle Buster handshake, pull back your hand and tell them their handshake is crazy and that they need to relax a little. Don't show pain because, in the event the intention was to dominate or impress you, that reaction feeds into their not-so-secret goal of overpowering you.

Try this handshake on some of your work colleagues. Note the reaction on their faces. Then ask what the handshake said to them. Now try doing it with a stranger and notice the reaction. Do they pull back or go along for the ride?

The Tug

Similar to the Controller, the Tug is more than a quick shake and release. With the Tug, the shaker uses the grip to pull you closer, usually to say something discreetly—a secret or a warning perhaps.

While grasping—no longer shaking—your hand, the Tugger might use his other hand to hold your arm or shoulder. It becomes more of a capture than a greeting, holding you in a position where you're somewhat trapped. The connection of your hands may seem like a friendly greeting to casual onlookers, but the Tug is meant to exert control and uses the handshake as a guise.

Look for examples of the Tug in a variety of situations. In a business environment, watch the expression on the face of the recipient of the handshake, the person who has been yanked into brief submission. Is he or she registering surprise? Concern? Frustration? Anger? Pay attention to this thinly veiled greeting because it always carries more than a friendly "hello."

The Politician

The Politician is one of those truly unique handshakes because it requires **both** hands. You shake firmly with your right hand and then put your left hand on top of the hand you're grasping. Sometimes, the second hand can grab hold of the wrist or forearm. The goal here is to communicate sincerity and exert influence, but it often has the opposite reaction, particularly if the rest of the shaker's body language doesn't put you at ease (darting eyes, pursed lips). The Politician handshake is a little over the top when you don't know the other person. If you receive this handshake from a stranger, they aren't likely to be genuine. If you really know this person well, then this two-handed greeting is very appropriate, particularly if you **aren't** a politician.

THE POLITICIAN

You can turn on the news anytime and see the current US president, past presidents, or politicians shaking hands, and it's almost always the same grip. In political debates, it's fun to watch the greeting between the candidates when they come onto the stage. You will probably witness a two-sided Politician's handshake, where both debaters grip with two hands. Watch the body language between the two contenders as they attempt to offer a warm greeting to one another. Is it genuine? Is it sincere? You be the judge.

The Dead Fish

This one really stinks! You think you are about to receive a nice handshake and—"Boom!"—you get a lifeless limb. The Dead Fish feels as if the person shaking your band has no bones in their hands. It's a weak, limp, emotionless blob of a handshake. If represented in a cartoon, the shaker would release the hand and the recipient would be looking shocked and disgusted at a dead fish in his palm.

> If you want to get elected, shake hands with 25,000 people between now and November 7.
>
> —Harry S. Truman

The person who serves up the Dead Fish handshake is usually a passive type and likely uncomfortable around other people. This isn't necessarily a bad thing, but the handshakes are unpleasant. As soft and lifeless as this shake is, the message it communicates is striking. A Dead Fish recipient will feel repulsed, offended or unimpressed.

I was recently on a flight and my boarding pass was accidentally switched with another passenger who had the same name as me. When I got on the plane, the attendant told me to exchange boarding passes with the other Michael Anthony so that we would have our correct seating. We met, laughed at our identical names, shook hands, and— "Boooya!"—I got the Dead Fish. He's not representing the name very well. Too bad. So sad.

First and foremost, a handshake is intended as a greeting. What message is a Dead Fish sending? If you're not sure, try using it on someone who will tell you like it is.

MICHAEL'S TIP

Remember that some people may not be amenable to a handshake. A person with arthritis, a hand injury, or fear of sharing germs might be better served with a friendly nod.

The Lobster Claw

Michael C. Anthony

Don't worry, this person won't really pinch you, but it's a unique handshake that you are sure to notice. With the Lobster Claw, the shaker uses only their fingers and thumb—no palm involved—and basically pinches your hand with what seems like a claw. A slightly different version of the Lobster Claw is Ladyfingers. There is minimal contact— just fingers, no palms, but without the pinch of the Claw. And you're not sure if you should shake the fingers or kiss the hand!

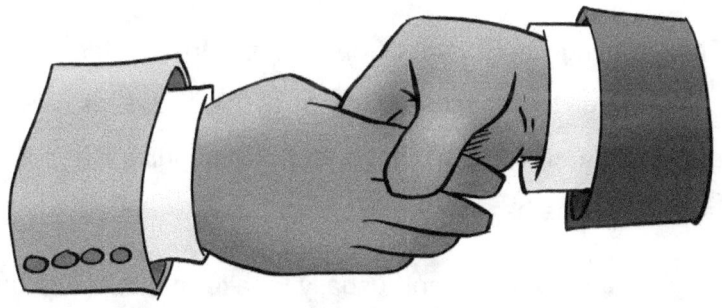

THE LOBSTER CLAW

People who use this type of handshake are attempting to avoid palm-to-palm contact, a sure sign that they may be insecure and/or don't want to get too close. Physical connection makes them uncomfortable. This person is often insecure and afraid of connecting.

When reading either of these finger shakes, consider the other body language clues. Observe the eye contact. If the person's eyes are looking down, he or she might be insecure. If looking away, they might be disinterested or feel superior to you. They are making the absolute minimum contact possible for a greeting.

But don't be too quick to judge; some people who get freaked out by germs may shake this way as well.

The Global Language of Handshakes

The greeting ritual varies from country to country. Some cultures don't use handshakes at all. Because we live in a multicultural world, it's important to recognize when and how to use the handshake.

- ✓ **Russians** do not usually shake hands with the opposite sex. It is considered rude for a man to shake a woman's hand.

- ✓ Certain **Middle Eastern** cultures do not use a firm handshake, so you shouldn't be offended when you don't receive a hearty shake in return.

✓ **Chinese** shake hands with a lighter grip, but they hold on for a longer time.

✓ When greeting a **Japanese** person, let them initiate the handshake, and don't grasp firmly when the hand is offered.

✓ **French** people shake hands when greeting and saying goodbye.

✓ **Germans** prefer one hand pump.

✓ The **Swiss** will shake a woman's hand first.

✓ **Filipinos** would rather text their hand shake to you with their cell phone. They text more than any country in the world per capita.

Palm reading

When offering your hand, the way you present your palm sends a message:

Vertical puts you on an equal level.

....

Facing down is a sign of superiority or dominance.

....

Facing up conveys submission.

....

Tilted slightly upward signifies humility or servant hood.

The Fist Bump

The fist bump isn't really a handshake at all. The fist bump is when one person offers a closed fist instead of an open hand and expects the other person will also extend their fists and they lightly bump their knuckles together. What does it mean? Well, it likely means the bumpers are young and possibly too hip for a traditional handshake. It may also mean that they aren't too interested in spreading germs which can be a big issue with traditional handshakes.

Have you even been to church during flu season and the minister asks everyone to turn and greet your neighbor. Can you say "hello, influenza?"

Handshakes are a bittersweet ritual that will be with us forever whether we like them or not, so be sure to carry your hand sanitizer the next time you greet some strangers at church.

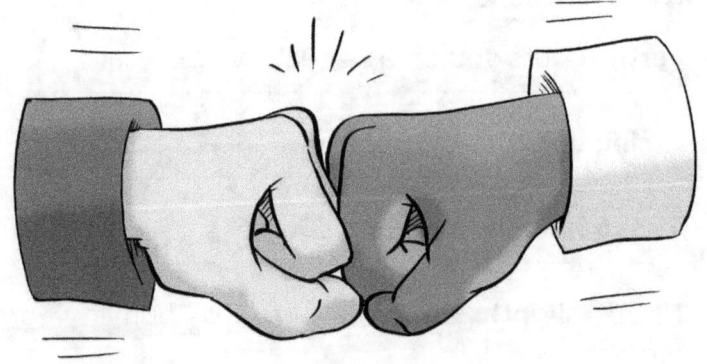

THE FIST BUMP

Back to the fist bump. This fist bump can also be accompanied with some other random moves including what people call the "explosion." This is when you bump fists and then spread out and wiggle your fingers to simulate an explosion. This is usually accompanied with a vocal sound of an explosion too. What does this mean? It means these fist bumpers are wackadoodles.

The Perfect Handshake

So, we've covered a wide variety of handshakes, each with their own meaning. If you simply want to offer a friendly greeting, what's the right way to shake someone's hand?

THE PERFECT HANDSHAKE

Well, it starts with eye contact and a pleasant smile. Offer your right hand with your open palm in a vertical position and the thumb up. Grasp the other person's hand firmly—not too strong or too weak. Shake up and down two or three times and let go, maintaining eye contact throughout. Simple and effective. It's even best to keep the eye contact for a couple seconds afterward, but don't get creepy.

Language Lab

✓ The next time you are at an event or event and you'll be shaking a lot of hands, pay close attention to the handshakes you receive and monitor if they are congruent with their personalities and positions.

✓ Watch the eye contact others make during the handshake and more importantly; be very aware of your own.

Heads Up—Eyes, Nose, Mouth, and Neck

> When the eyes say one thing and the tongue another,
> a practiced man relies on the language of the first.
>
> —Ralph Waldo Emerson

"La plume de ma tante."

"Que pasa?"

"Arigato."

You might know what these phrases mean. You might not. You might also know how to say certain things in different languages.

But that doesn't make you fluent.

Back when President Jimmy Carter was visiting Poland, he had the help of linguists, but when he attempted to say. "I have a strong desire to know the Polish people", it actually came out as "I desire the Polish people carnally."

When Pepsi-Cola launched a new campaign in China, the literal translation of the slogan, "Come alive with the Pepsi generation" turned out to be "Pepsi brings back your dead ancestors."

You simply can't take a little bit of knowledge and assume you're communicating effectively. Non-verbal communication can range from an almost imperceptible facial movement to a broad, sweeping gesture. In order to best interpret the meaning, you need to treat it like any language. A gesture is a word. A combination of gestures is a sentence. So, I'm going to teach you how to conjugate the non-verbal verbs so you can better understand the subtlety of body language.

Just like a detective wouldn't rely on one clue to assess the guilt of a suspect, you shouldn't rely on one or two non-verbal signals to jump to a conclusion.

Let's Face It

The eyes are the windows to the soul, right? Your mouth may say, "No!" but your eyes say, "Yes! Yes!" When you also add in the motions of the nose, mouth, and jaw, you have a lot of body language going on.

Facial expressions combine a broad variety of movement—wrinkling your nose while grimacing, crinkling your eyes while smiling, flaring your nostrils as your eyes pop wide open. So, there are many ways to read a face.

Let's start with six universal facial expressions:

Which face shows happiness? Sadness? Fear? Disgust? Surprise? Anger?

1. HAPPINESS—SIGNIFIED BY SMILING

2. SADNESS—SIGNIFIED BY FROWNING

3. FEAR—RAISED EYEBROWS, WIDE-OPEN EYES, MOUTH SLIGHTLY OPEN

4. DISGUST—RAISED UPPER LIP, WRINKLED BRIDGE OF THE NOSE

5. SURPRISE-ARCHED BROWS, EYES OPEN WIDE TO EXPOSE WHITE, DROPPED JAW

6. ANGER-LOWERED BROWS, LIPS PRESSED FIRMLY TOGETHER, BULGING EYES

Each expression is identified by a variety of facial gestures, not just one. Every individual will have his or her own variation for the expression. Some people, for example, try to hold back a smile; others mask their anger. So, while some expressions are obvious, you might have to do a little more looking when reading people who are guarded with their emotions—or more in tune with their body language.

Let's now gain some "vocabulary" by breaking down the expressions into specific facial areas.

The Eyes

Eye contact plays a huge part in understanding body language. You can connect with someone from across a room just by looking into one another's eyes. You can shoot the "come hither" stare or the "dagger eyes" just by the way you use your eyes, lids and brows. You can look at a person who has the "deer in the headlights" gaze and know they are clueless or totally disinterested. Or a quick wink between two people tells anyone who is watching that there's something secret going on.

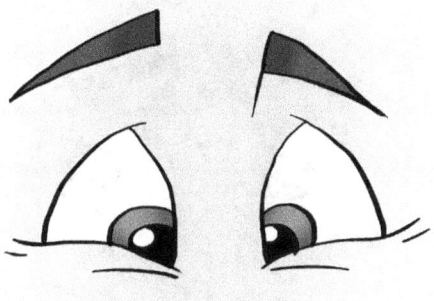

HAPPY EYES

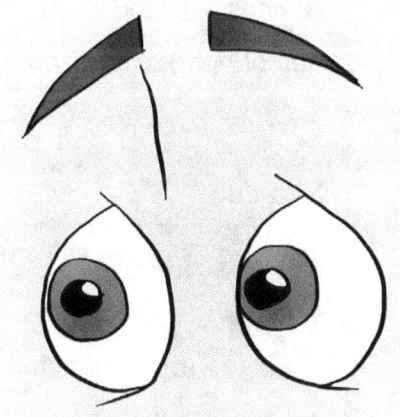

SURPRISED EYES

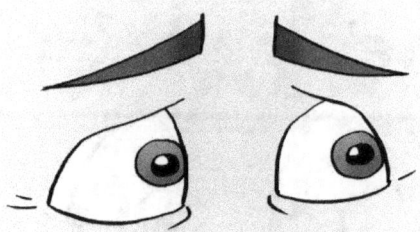

WORRIED EYES

Here's a glossary of eye movements and gestures, along with the potential meanings. Oh, and just to be clear, when I indicate a direction (left or right), I'm referring to the person who is making the movement, not the one who is seeing it.

Movement	Meaning
Looking to the side	*Annoyed, disinterested.* This person is avoiding eye contact with you—either to avoid confrontation or faking niceties. Or, the peripheral vision has caught something distracting and there's a quick sideways glance to see what it is.

Looking side to side	*Nervous, lying.* Beware. The eyes are looking for a way out of this conversation.
Looking up and right	*Lying, guessing, fabricating.* The eyes shift to the right when accessing the right side of the brain, which controls creative thought. The person is trying to come up with a response, as opposed to recalling a fact.
Looking down and right	*Self-questioning.* The person is trying to think through their thoughts and feelings.
Looking up and left	*Remembering.* Conversely, when looking to the left, the person is guided by the left side of the brain, which controls linear thinking. They're reaching into their mental fact file.
Looking down and left	*Self-talk.* Rather than contemplating an emotion (as in looking down and to the right), the person is pondering an outward decision (weighing facts).

Looking down	*Guilt, submission.* Lowering the eyes is either a wordless admission of guilt or an act of deference.
Eye contact when speaking	*Honesty* Unless the person is a master of self-control, direct eye contact when speaking is a good sign of truthfulness. That's why you hear people say, "Look me in the eye and say it."
Eye contact when listening	*Interest, attention, attraction.* Strong eye contact is a sign that the listener is focused and interested in what you're saying.
Dilated pupils	*Attraction, desire.* Sexual attraction causes the pupils to enlarge. But a lot of light will have the same effect, so don't get too amorous if you're outside and looking into the eyes of someone whose eyes are merely reacting to the daylight.

Squinting	*Doubt, suspicion, stress, or anger.* Clint Eastwood was a master of the squint in his movies and could convey more with one eye movement than a long speech. For everyone else, a squint means they're weighing up what you're saying, possibly getting angry over it—or the sun is too bright or they need glasses!
Winking	*Friendly, complicit.* The winker may be offering a friendly gesture or asking you to keep a secret.
Half-closed	*Bored, tired.* When a person is alert and attentive, their eyes are open. Dropping eyelids is a sign that they are not paying attention—whether tired, bored or both.
Wide open	*Excited, surprised, interested.* The eyes pop open when there's a jolt to the mind—like a news flash. When coupled with raised eyebrows, the meaning escalates to surprise at a shock level.

Rolling eyes	*Annoyance.* If you've got a teenager, you've seen this look. The infamous eye roll—as in "you sooo don't understand!"
Frequent blinking	*Excited, nervous.* The average person blinks their eyes between 6 and 20 times per minute. The rate increases with excitement or anxiousness—often caused when someone is being dishonest or trying to hide something. Of course, don't confuse a fast blink rate with batting the eyes, which is a flirtatious gesture.
Rubbing	*Fatigue, frustration, annoyance.* Unless the individual is clearly trying to wake up or rubbing goop out of his eyes, you can safely assume that he is trying to rub out the frustration or annoyance while avoiding making eye contact with you.

Raised eyebrow	*Fear, surprise, acknowledgement, doubt.* One raised eyebrow usually signifies doubt, but a double lift is likely to be fear or surprise—unless accompanied by a slight nod, which is acknowledging your presence.
Furrowed eyebrows	*Anger, anxiety, concentration.* Some people wrinkle up their brows when they're deeply focused—and they look angry. Be careful to gage the attitude here before you rush to the conclusion that a furrowed brow signals a negative emotion.

The Nose Knows

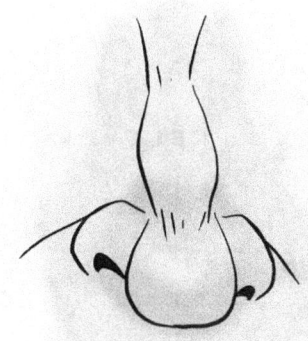

Your nose functions to process smells, but as a facial feature, it contributes non-verbal cues. From the flare of your nostrils to touching your nose in certain ways, you deliver distinct "tells". By paying attention to these clues, you will know what the nose knows.

Movement	Meaning
Wrinkled nose	*Disgust.* Whether offended by an unpleasant odor or an unpleasant person, this person is displaying a degree of displeasure.
Flared nostrils	*Anger.* The nose is used for breathing and when we need to take in more oxygen, the nostrils flare. It's also linked to the fight-or-flight response. Inhaling in this way prepares for a fight—much like the bull ready to charge!
Pinching the bridge	*Contemplation, frustration.* In some cases, the individual is pinching her nose to shield her eyes and avoid visual distraction in order to concentrate. In other instances, this pinch is a sign of annoyance.

Rubbing	*Uncertainty, disagreement.* Stroking the nose could mean that the person doesn't believe what you're saying or disagrees—a strong clue that you need to step up your game!
Touching	*Lying.* Touching the side of the nose is often a sign that the speaker is not telling the truth or withholding information.
Picking	*Disconnected.* Unless the picker has a real itch or something just flew up there, nose picking as a habit is a sign of inattentiveness. The mind is drifting off and the fingers, in need of something to explore, head for the sinus cavity. Gross!

MICHAEL'S TIP

Look in the mirror and get a look at what you'd consider your "work face" is it too sad, serious or stressed? If so, make a conscious change in your face because it will change your state, Plus, you never knows who's looking.

The Mouth

It's not always what comes **out** of your mouth that matters. As the only part of your body that can deliver both verbal and non-verbal messages, your mouth is highly communicative! You can listen to what's being said, but don't overlook what isn't.

Movement	Meaning
Closed lip smile	*Pleased.* This is one of those pleasant, polite smiles. The lips are closed—but not pursed—and no teeth are showing. It might be merely an acknowledgement, accompanied with a slight nod.

Slightly open smile	*Happy.* The upper teeth are showing, indicating genuine pleasure—assuming the lips aren't stretched into a pasted smile, which is masking another feeling.
Broad smile	*Joy.* This full-out smile shows all your teeth and may cause your eyes to crinkle ("laughing eyes").
Smiling grimace	*Pretense, insincerity.* The teeth are clenched together and the lips are slightly parted and pulled back, creating a forced smile that could just as easily be a grimace. The expression is faked pleasantry, like when two political candidates greet one another.
Pasted smile	*Pretense, insincerity.* This forced smile is similar to the smiling grimace, but it might appear less pained. Still, it seems stuck on the face as the person is fighting to maintain a happy façade. Be assured, it's all a pretense to mask true feelings.

Tight-lipped smile	*Secretive.* The lips are zipped, holding back information.
Pursed lips	*Concentration, frustration.* Tightly pressed lips are a sign that a person is frustrated, holding back words or in deep thought. When combined with flared nostrils, it's more likely to be frustration.
Pout	*Disappointment, flirtation.* When the lower lip juts out, it means that the person either didn't get what she wanted or is playfully teasing. You be the judge, based on the context.
Biting lip	*Nervous, insecure, embarrassed, focused.* One bite usually signals embarrassment; chewing on the lip is more likely to reflect nerves. Some people bite or chew their lips (or stick out the tongue slightly) when they are in deep concentration.

Licking lips	*Attraction, nervous.* Slow licking doesn't necessarily mean that lip-licker is flirting with you. He or she might just be eyeing the tempting dessert on the table behind you. Continual licking is a sure sign of nerves.
Tongue poking out	*Disapproval.* From just the tip protruding between the lips to the full tongue sticking out, the gesture indicates distaste.
Hand over mouth	*Lying.* When poised with the hand over the mouth and the thumb on the cheek, the brain is subconsciously trying to keep the mouth from spewing false words.
Finger in mouth	*Insecure, doubtful, nervous.* Unless you're enjoying some finger-licking good chicken, nibbling on a fingertip or knuckle is a sure sign of uncertainty or concern.

Head, Neck, and Face

We've zeroed in on the telling signs of the eyes, nose, and mouth, so let's spread out a little. From the tilt of the head to a stroke of the chin, the gestures happening above the shoulders are sending you useful clues about a person's mindset.

Movement	Meaning
Head tilt	*Interest.* When someone is listening to you with a slightly tilted head, he's interested in what you're saying.
Head tilt, prolonged	*Boredom.* If the head tilt lasts for an extended period, it signals boredom. Wrap up what you're saying and move on, because you're losing your audience!
Head tilt with a smile	*Playful, flirtatious.* Add the joy associated with the smile and conjugate with a head tilt, and you have a playful demeanor. Throw in a little hair toss, and it's most definitely flirtation.

Head tilt downward	*Disapproval, disagreement.* When a person doesn't make eye contact, there's usually a negative connotation. During a conversation, this downward focus means the person doesn't like what you're saying.
Nodding	*Agreement, understanding.* We nod to indicate a non-verbal "yes"
Slow nodding	*Attentive.* Slowly moving the head up and down is the listener's way of acknowledging they're hearing you.
Fast nodding	*Impatience.* This is the non-verbal equivalent of "Yes, yes, I get it. Move on, will ya?"
Shaking back and forth	*Disagreement.* The (almost) universal sign for "no"—as in "no", "you're wrong", and "no way!"
Head held high	*Pride, superiority.* Unless you're balancing something on your head, this upright manner tells the world you are confident in yourself— possibly overly confident.

Chin up	*Pride, defiant, confident.* The jutting chin can be like a challenge. It says, "I dare you!"
Head jutted forward	*Interest.* Spatially, a forward pushing head is leaning in without bringing the rest of the body, so the gesture definitely communicates interest. If coupled with wide eyes, the body language here says surprise.
Head down when listening	*Disinterested.* Good listening is accompanied by eye contact. A listener averts her eyes when she is distracted or disinterested.
Head down during action	*Tired, defeated.* Okay, I'm not talking about your golf swing here, but if you're walking around with your head drooping, you're telling the world that you're not at your best.
Rubbing chin	*Thoughtful, contemplative.* This is gentle stroking, like when you're pondering your next move in a chess match.

Scratching neck	*Doubt.* Often accompanied by the verbal "Gee, I don't know. Let me think about it and get back to you."
Rubbing neck	*Frustration, tension, deceit.* Rubbing an open palm along the back of the neck is a self-soothing gesture.
Tugging ear	*Indecision, self-comfort.* Reaching for the ear, whether rubbing or tugging, is a clue that the individual is thinking and that those thoughts require comfort or a challenging decision.
Touching throat	*Uncomfortable, nervous, lying.* Most assuredly a gesture to show discomfort, touching the throat could reflect the person's anxiety about the person they're speaking with or the situation. Some individuals react this way when meeting a celebrity or someone they find attractive. On the other hand, throat touching can be a sign that the person is trying to cover up a lie.

Covering throat	*Threatened, insecure.* The throat is perhaps the most vulnerable part of your body, so reaching up and placing your hand over your throat is an instinctive reaction to a perceived threat. The center area of the throat (the part that has a small divot.) is called the suprasternal notch. You've likely seen people (frequently when telling a lie) protect this area with a light massage. Often, a woman will play with her necklace or a man will adjust his tie. This is where we get the term "hot under the collar." More about lying later.
Removing glasses	*Seeking acknowledgement.* When a person removes his glasses, he is usually preparing to make a statement or shifting into a more serious mode.

Practice Makes Perfect

Your body language vocabulary is building. Build your fluency by looking for the telltale signs in the eyes, nose, mouth, face, and head. Make a note of what you see and if your perception matches the definitions provided here.

Armed and Dangerous

> The language of the body is the key that can
> unlock the soul.
>
> —Konstantin Stanislavsky

Your facial body language may be excellent. Maybe you make great eye contact and your lips, nose, and jaw are doing everything right. Is it possible that the rest of your body may be telling a different story?

Body language is about the whole body. As I've mentioned, the more clues you gather from a person's non-verbal communication, the more reliable your interpretation.

In this chapter, we'll work through the language of the arms, shoulders, hands, legs, feet and posture. I'm also going to give you some help in understanding the meaning of proxemics, a fancy word for personal space. When you can interpret the individual parts of the body's movements, you can conjugate a full body language sentence, paragraph, and story!

The Hands

Hands deliver the most noticeable messages—from waving goodbye to flipping off a rude driver. A baseball catcher uses finger signals to advise the pitcher which pitch to throw. Anyone who has ever hailed a cab knows that the choice of hand wave is essential. Whether you're showing the guy at the deli counter how thin you want your meat cut, pointing out a roadside attraction, or giving the thumbs up sign, you use your hands to communicate messages.

You use your hands and fingers to touch, pat, stroke, pick, flick, grab, squeeze, and pinch. There are 27 bones and 20 muscles, plus nerves, tendons and ligaments that enable your hand to be so flexible.

While some body parts are stuck in place—eyes, ears, and nose—your hands can reach out and touch, which opens up another section of body language. Whether you're tugging your ear, scratching your nose or patting someone on the arm, your hands can deliver the broadest range of non-verbal messages.

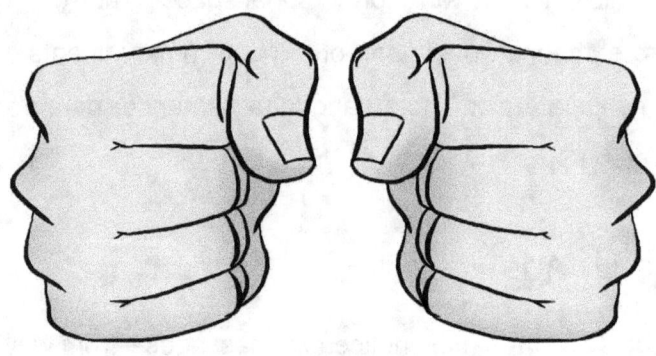

CLOSED FISTS CAN MEAN DETERMINATION, STRESS, HIDING SOMETHING OR ANGER.

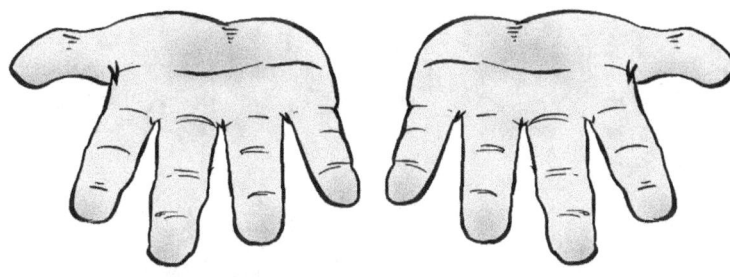

OPEN, UPWARD PALMS SAY, "I'M AN OPEN BOOK",
"I'M HONEST", "I'M HERE TO SERVE".

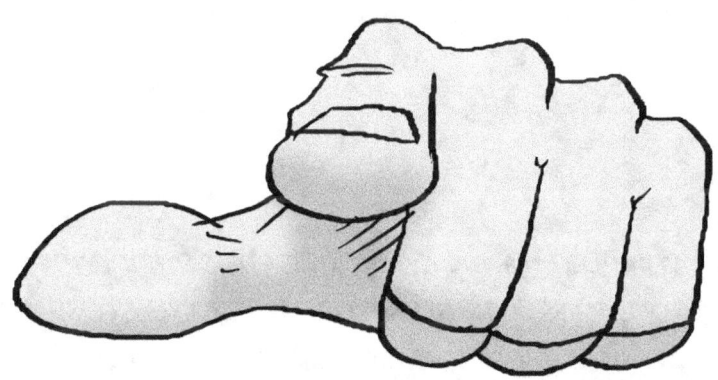

A POINTED FINGER CAN MEAN THE SPEAKER IS
DRIVING A POINT HOME OR POSSIBLY TELLING A LIE.

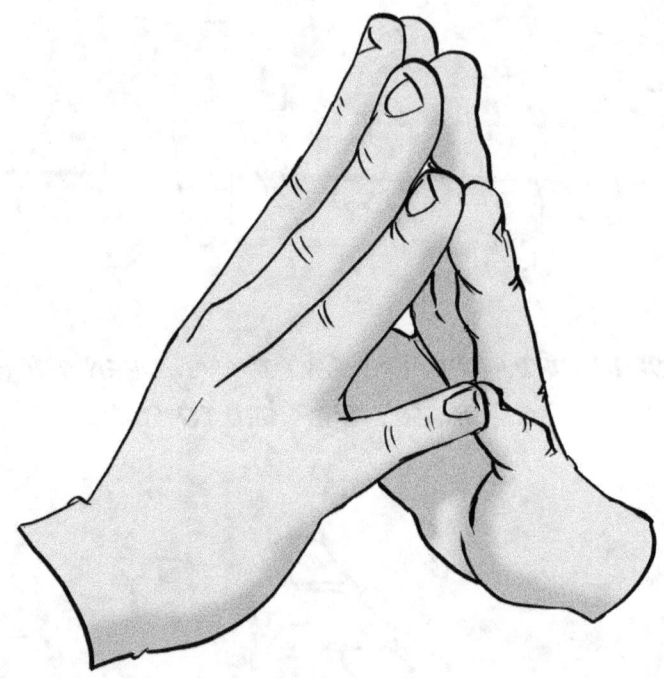

STEEPLED HANDS COMMUNICATE CONFIDENCE, KNOWLEDGE AND EXPERTISE. STEEPLING CLOSE TO THE FACE IS AN INTIMIDATION TACTIC.

I'm not going to try to cover the various meaning of common, obvious gestures, like a wave, "OK" sign, thumbs up or pinky swear. Instead, I want you to learn the clues that you might be missing.

Movement	Meaning
Palm(s) up or open	*Honesty, submissiveness, pleading.* Just like the handshake evolved from soldiers showing they carried no weapons, the open hand is a gesture of openness and honesty. By exposing your palms, you're showing trust, truthfulness, or vulnerability.
Palm(s) down	*Disagreement, domination.* Contrary to the open hands, this gesture is the hands way of showing that the mind is mentally pushing down on the person being addressed.
Open palms facing downward, moving up and down	*Seeking control.* When voices are raised or events seem to be spiraling out of control, this gesture is the mind's way of attempting to put a lid on it.
Open palms facing upward, moving up and down	*Contemplating.* While the mind is weighing a problem or pondering a decision, the hands are creating a visual scale.

Steepled fingers, fingertips pointing up	*Thoughtfulness, confidence* When the fingertips on opposite hands are touching, the person is contemplating—or at least, trying to communicate that message. If the hands come up and to the face, this person may be trying to intimidate you.
Steepled fingers, fingertips pointing forward	*Directed thoughtfulness, confidence., knowledgeable.* The steepled fingers indicate the person is thinking, but when the fingertips point forward, there's direction to the thought. It can be accusatory or just guiding the listener.
Open hand chop downward	*Emphasis, control.* The speaker is making a cut like a karate chop to drive home a point or put an end to the discussion point. Think of it like, "I have spoken. The end."
Hands on hips	*Readiness, aggression.* Not quite ready to strike, this individual is chomping at the bit to get moving.

Clenched fist, thumb out	*Anger, aggression.* A clenched fist waved in your face is an overt threat, while a person clenching a fist with his arm at his side it attempting to harness his rising anger.
Clenched fist, thumb in	*Insecurity, worry, frustration.* Wrapping the thumb in a protective-like gesture is not outwardly threatening, but inwardly protective.
Knuckle cracking	*Self-comforting, threatening.* Unless the knuckle-cracker is extending the palms of his hands in your direction, you can take the action to mean the person is seeking to calm down and comfort himself, like a sort of muscle stretch.
Massaging hands	*Tense, anxious.* This gesture is self-comforting. One hand is trying to relax the other. The rubbing is attempting to push away the nervous energy.

Rubbing open hands together	*Anticipation.* This action gleefully says, "Let's go. I'm ready. Bring it on!"
Fiddling with cuff or watch	*Nervous.* The nervous impulse moves from the brain to the extremities, which results in fiddling fingers or jiggling feet.
Playing with wedding ring	*Relationship uncertainty.* Twisting the wedding ring in the presence of another person can be a sign of attraction. Fiddling with the ring in this way is an unconscious way of dealing with the commitment that feels like a restraint.
Picking at someone's lint or clothes	*Disapproval.* Plucking the lint off someone's jacket, smoothing the collar on their shirt, or adjusting their clothes in some way signifies disapproval of the individual. It's an attempt to reshape the person.

Hands in pockets	*Insecure.* This gesture is the mind's way of finding a place to hide. The hands are very communicative so hiding them away is a sign of closure. It shows the desire not to communicate with another person. The pocket protector may be unsure or uncomfortable in a situation or with another person. When combined with certain other clues—like lack of eye contact—the thing that the person could be hiding is the truth.
Hands in pockets, thumbs out	*Confident, superior.* The thumb is a conveyor of superiority, so when the hands are hidden but the thumbs are outside the pocket, the person is indicating he is confident in himself and possibly feeling above you. In the mating/dating world, the person with the thumbs out is showing a sign of dominance.

Thumbs hooked in pockets	*Confident, superior.* As with the thumbs-only pocket tuck (above), the position of the thumbs communicates the sign of superiority. When those digits alone are finding their way into the pocket, the person is comfortable, confident and feeling pretty darn good about himself.
Holding a cup or other object with one hand	*Comfort.* Holding onto a coffee cup, for example, provides an outer connection and is akin to hugging oneself.
Holding something with two hands	*Nervous.* Using both hands creates a barrier with the arms. The coffee mug, particularly when held at chest level, is establishing a boundary between the individual with the cup and anyone else nearby.

Fidgeting hands	*Nervous, impatient.* Incessantly tapping a pencil on a table or clicking a pen is an outward expression of nervous energy.
Tugging the collar	*Nervous, angry.* Pulling at the collar is a subconscious attempt to get more air—either to inhale or for cooling comfort. The individual is feeling constrained by an uncomfortable situation and trying to find a release.

MICHAEL'S TIP

If you want to instantly convey confidence and wisdom, put your hands together and STEEPLE, PEOPLE!

The Arms and Shoulders

The hands rely on the arms to get them where they want to go, but a simple movement of an elbow or shrug of the shoulder can be a valuable clue as to a person's demeanor. The arms can spread wide to make you larger or wrap around your body to close you in and protect you. Pay attention to the position and movement from the shoulder all the way down to the wrists for these distinguishing "tells".

Movement	Meaning
Crossed arms	*Confident, defensive, bored.* This one is tricky depending on the situation. It's important to look at the surroundings before you make an assumption. Is this person a boss or an expert of some type? If so they may be crossing their arms as a confident gesture. Is the arm-crosser in a difficult situation? Maybe he is being told he did an inferior job on his last report? If so, he is crossing his arms as a defensive, self-soothing gesture. Two people opposite one another, each with their arms crossed, is a stand-off. The walls are up and no one is budging! So, get a feel for what may be going on before you judge the arm-crosser. It's also important to understand the arm-crosser that is in a sitting position may simply be comfortable—or even cold.

Crossed arms with clenched fists	*Aggression.* This non-verbal signal combines the aggressiveness of the fists with the defensive posture of the folded arms. Consider it like a growling dog warning you to stay back.
One arm across body and gripping opposite arm	*Nervous.* Another protective gesture that says, "Keep your distance. I'm not too sure about you."
Clutching something in front of body	*Nervous, insecure.* From holding a book, stack of folders or a handbag, the gesture of clutching anything in front of your chest is a protective measure that signals uncertainty—or a mustard stain.
Arms behind back, hands clasped	*Confident.* Leaving your front open and vulnerable is a sure sign of trust and confidence.
Arms behind back, one hand gripping opposite wrist	*Frustration.* One arm is holding the other, in a subconscious gesture of self-control.

Arms crossed behind head, hands clasped	*Confident, relaxed.* This posture leaves a person fully exposed, which indicates trust, comfort, security and confidence.
Arms behind back, one hand gripping the other	*Confident, superior.* With the body exposed, the person is confident enough to feel safe and unthreatened. With this posture, the shoulders are also pulled back, adding to the confident air.
Shoulders back	*Confidence.* Standing tall and erect leaves the torso open, which is the ultimate sign of confidence.
Slouched shoulders	*Insecure, dejected.* The mind is carrying a huge weight and the shoulders show the burden.
Shrug	*Doubt, indifference, confusion.* A shrug needs to be read in context with the situation and other gestures, particularly in the face. It can mean, "I don't know", "I don't care" or "I'm not being honest." A quick shrug is almost like a reflexive volley, shooting a wordless response and hoping it lands.

The Legs and Feet

The body language of the legs and feet can easily be missed, because they're not as readily seen as face, arm, and hand movements, unless you're sitting down. Your lower extremities represent your support. Think of your legs and feet as your body's compass. Your feet will point in the direction of your interest when you're standing. When sitting down, your legs and knees are directed in the area where your mind is really focused.

Movement	Meaning
Standing with legs straight and together	*Respectful, attentive.* Here's the classic "At attention!" posture, when coupled with arms and hands at your side and shoulders straight or back. From a physiological standpoint, it's great posture. In body language, it can communicate respectful attention and submissiveness.
Standing with legs a shoulder's width apart	*Comfortable.* This position provides good balance and indicates that a person is relaxed and comfortable in the situation.

Standing with legs splayed	*Dominant.* The spread legs are marking a broader personal space, like territory. Just think Superheroes.
Standing with legs far apart and hips forward	*Dominant.* This is more commonly a male posture, where the pelvic thrust is either sending out a sexual attraction signal or conveying male dominance.
Standing with one foot forward	*Readiness.* Having your feet apart provides balance but when one foot is forward, it shows the desire to move ahead. Be sure to notice where the foot is pointing to determine the intended direction.
Standing with one knee bent	*Pressured.* The weight of a particular burden is showing itself with the knee giving way slightly. The stress could be from anxiousness, indecision, or another issue. Look at the facial cues to determine the meaning more accurately.

Standing with legs crossed	*Insecure, submissive.* Like the crossed arms, this posture creates a protective barrier.
Sitting with legs uncrossed	*Open, relaxed.* Much like standing with your hands at your side, you're allowing your extremities to be in an open position with no barriers.
Sitting with legs and knees together	*Propriety.* At some point, you're probably taught that this is the polite sitting position, but we all know it's not comfortable. Those who assume this seating posture are trying to communicate a sense of good manners and propriety.
Sitting with legs crossed at the knee	*Guarded.* Crossing the legs is another barrier position. It is often combined with various other clues, like the pointing toe, jiggling foot, or bouncing knee. Be sure to note where the knee and foot are pointing, because this direction signals the true area of the person's interest.

Sitting with legs crossed and bouncing foot or knee	*Anxious.* When an extremity, like the hand or foot, is bouncing or jiggling, it is carrying the outward signs of nervousness, like the dead end where the brain's messages can't go any farther.
Sitting with legs crossed at ankles	*Relaxed.* The feet are either forward or to the side. By not crossing at the knees, the individual feels no need for barriers.
Crossed ankles tucked back	*Anxious.* This is a protective posture, like hiding hands in a pocket.
Sitting with Figure-4 leg cross	*Stubborn, independent.* The legs are crossed with one ankle balanced on the opposite knee, creating something like a number four. The sitter is creating a frame around the genital area, communicating strong confidence, which can escalate to stubbornness.

Sitting with Figure-4 leg cross with ankle grab	*Stubborn.* In this position, one hand is holding onto the ankle of the crossed leg. It's a closed position, signifying that the person is holding tight to his ideas, beliefs, or statement.
Sitting with twisted legs	*Insecure, interest.* The legs are not just crossed; they're wound around each other, like a clinging vine. It could be a protective gesture, like wrapping your arms around yourself, but if combined with signals like a smile, hair flick or slight head tilt, the pretzel legs could be communicating sexual interest.

Posture

The spine is the center of your nervous system. It's one of the first parts of the body to develop. Literally your backbone, the spine carries the weight of your body. A weak spine causes health problems and limits your movement. When you stand tall, you strengthen your spine. Slouch, and you lose the strength of your backbone.

Posture is a body language cue that can range from subtle to blatant. Your shoulders might droop a little, or you could look like your carrying a half-ton weight on your back, with a full slouch. The taller you stand, the more confidence you exude. Hunching over—unless you're working on something that requires you to bend that much—shows defeat and lack of confidence.

OUR POSTURE SAYS A LOT ABOUT US.

Ballroom dancers sometimes work with a strengthening bar to improve their frame. They put a rod behind their neck and drape each arm over the ends. This position pulls back their shoulders and straightens their back. If you're feeling like you need a lift, grab a broom handle or baseball bat and give it a try!

A Dose of Reality

Practicing body language is best practiced by "people watching." The good news is that people are everywhere—in restaurants, airports, and at family gatherings. One way to simply watch the body language of others is reality TV. I realize a lot of reality TV has nothing at all to do with reality, but usually even the cast and producers of these shows don't know enough about body language to hide their true emotions with their bodies. The truth will usually shine through the bodies.

I enjoy a show called "Shark Tank". In some parts of the world it's called "Dragon's Den". It's a show where entrepreneurs with a new product or service pitch their idea to four judges (successful entrepreneurs) called "Sharks" or "Dragons." If these judges like the product or idea, they will compete with one another and invest their own money in the business concept.

Some of these business ideas are downright ridiculous and entertaining, while others are very clever. The entrepreneur may even have some past sales to entice the Sharks.

The interesting thing about the program to me, is watching the body language of these Sharks. When they see an idea they like, they adjust their positions. They go from a passive position to a proactive position. Their bodies lean forward, their heads tilt and their chins rise.

If they truly like the new business concept, then it's time to negotiate a deal with the entrepreneur. At this point, you watch the body language of these Sharks change again. They take on a more dominant, confident persona. The hands often come up to a steepling position. Steepling can mean confidence, dominance, or even intimidation (if the steeple is held high to the face or chin).

Many times, you'll see the Sharks shift their bodies to a position where they try to mask their true feelings. They try to hide the fact that they like the product, in order to give them more power during the negotiations. You'll see them touch their faces or noses, because they are trying to hide. You'll see them break eye contact and appear to write something on their pad of paper. You'll also see them turning to look at the other Sharks in an attempt to interpret what they are thinking.

It's fun to watch the entrepreneurs as well. You see dreams realized and hopes crumble. Try watching these shows with the volume muted. You'll still know exactly what's happening simply by watching their bodies.

Other "reality" shows like American Idol and The Voice and many more are great examples on how you can learn to read the minds of others, simply by reading their bodies.

Space Invasion

> Body language is a very powerful tool.
> We had body language before we had speech.
>
> —Deborah Bull

You've met them. The "Close Talkers" and the "Grand Canyons"—people who clearly define their comfort zone for personal space. The first one gets so close when speaking to you that you can identify what they ate that day. The second person is that individual who doesn't want to stand too close to other people, causing you to ask, "Excuse me, are you in line?" Invariably, you get the look of annoyance.

"Proxemics" is the technical term for **personal space**. In body language, the amount of space you leave between yourself and others can be as telling as your gestures and movements.

Think about sitting at a round dinner table with a group of people. Each of you has a space, defined by your place setting. If you move your glass or plate to your right, you're invading that diner's space. Try this the next time you're in such a situation: Move something toward the person next to you, just a few inches at a time, not all at once. See how close you get before that person nudges it away. That defines the edge of their comfort zone!

EACH OF US HAS DIFFERENT COMFORT LEVELS REGARDING OUR PERSONAL SPACE.

Spaced Out

Edward T. Hall, the American anthropologist who first coined the term "proxemics", defined four categories for space between people:

1
Intimate

Less than 6 inches to 18 inches. Used for touching, kissing, hugging, and whispering, such closeness shows a high degree of trust in this vulnerable proximity. "Intimate" doesn't necessarily mean "sexual". When you lean over to whisper in someone's ear at a meeting, you are stepping into the Intimate zone.

2
Personal

1.5 to 4 feet. This is the space allowed for familiar people, like friends, family, and some colleagues. You would feel comfortable within this range talking with people at a party, because you don't feel threatened or guarded. Obviously, there will be occasions where people in your inner circle also cross over to the Intimate zone.

3
Social

4 to 12 feet. When interacting with general acquaintances such as neighbors, colleagues, clients, and service providers— you will likely stay within this range, allowing conversation, but not touching. A salesperson should respect this boundary, at least until familiarity has been established.

4
Public

12 to 25 feet. Whether speaking to a group or just wandering about in public, you have a comfort zone with boundaries for the approach of strangers.

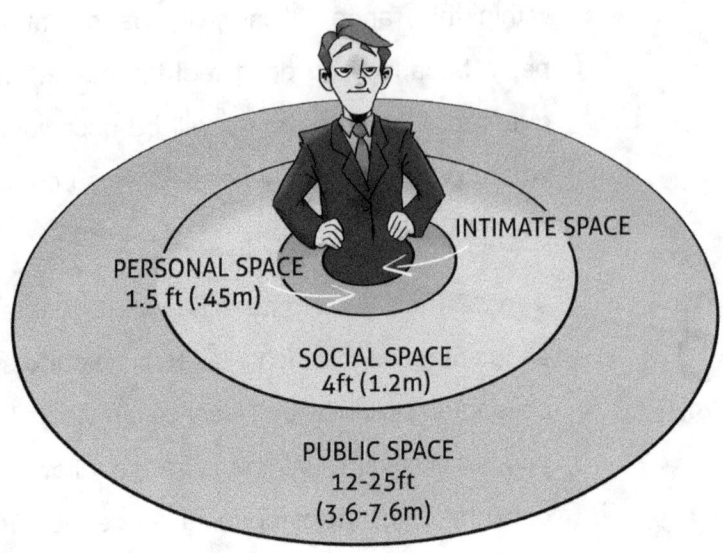

A Couple of "But's"

In order to become fluent in proxemics, you need to understand the factors that spark exceptions to these rules.

Cultural differences can affect the acceptable range of a zone. The distances defined here reflect North American, northern European, and Australian cultures. Edward T. Hall categorized cultural behavior by the way they interact:

LINEAR-ACTIVE

Cool and decisive, like people from the United States, Norway, Germany

REACTIVE

Accommodating and non-confrontational, such as Asian countries

MULTI-ACTIVE

Warm and impulsive, including Italy and Latin American countries

People from France, Italy, Greece, and Latin American countries are generally comfortable with closer personal space, while Asians and some Europeans (e.g., Brits) choose a wider gap. Because the Chinese and Japanese prefer a bow to a handshake, they naturally leave a little more space to avoid a cranial collision. Middle Easterners, however, often get right in your face! Before you violate someone's personal space or react to it yourself, stop and think about the possible cultural factor. If you're trying to do business with a Japanese company and you keep over-stepping the boundaries, that non-verbal conflict will turn potential opportunity into an undone deal!

Also, don't confuse your comfortable space with a forced one, like standing in line at a movie theater or on a crowded subway platform or talking with the stranger sitting next to you on an airplane. Unless you have an uncontrollable phobia, you can put your personal space lines on hold when a situation closes in on you. The mind's protective solution is to avoid eye contact, like in a crowded elevator when people stare at the numbers, door, or their shoes.

Mark Your Territory

The four personal space zones mark bodily boundaries, but proxemics also includes other ways to define your space, like your bedroom, office, or the coffee shop where you go every day. Humans are territorial creatures and we instinctively protect the people and places that matter to us. From securing our homes to protecting our reserved parking space, we subconsciously mark our territories:

1

Body

Obviously, the most personal of your territory, you will instinctively protect your body. That could mean reaching up and blocking something thrown at you, blocking your ears from loud noise, and jumping out of a crosswalk when a driver using a cell phone doesn't see you.

2
Primary

Your home sweet home is your most cherished territory, next to your body. This is your private habitat, a place not to be violated by burglars, home invaders or uninvited in-laws.

3
Secondary

This territory is familiar to you, like your workplace, school or church. You and all the people who go to these particular places follow a set of behavioral rules so that you can co-exist in this comfortable space.

4
Public

The wide, open spaces can range from a park or beach to a shopping mall or stadium. Anyone can go and the only limits are the laws of the land.

To mark your territory, you lay out personal belongings to create boundaries. This could be setting up your blanket on the beach, laying your jacket or bag on an empty chair or spreading your books or place setting on a table. If someone came along and moved any of these items without asking, your space would be violated.

Fight or Flight?

People who lack self-awareness often violate the Intimate or Personal zones of other people. The Close Talker, for example, will always get closer than what is considered a comfortable and acceptable distance. The Ringmaster is the person who gestures so broadly that you have to dodge and weave to avoid getting smacked. The Touchy-Feely person puts a hand on your shoulder or arm when talking, which is a sign of ownership or flirtation. Often, they don't feel the subtle flinch of the person being touched, but they can't overlook a noticeable jerking when you pull back.

Social and Public zone violations trigger interesting reactions and can make for a great sociological study, because the way a person responds to the space invasion tells a lot about their personality.

Just for fun—and research—I will look around a waiting room or airport gate and seek out the person who sits far apart from everyone else. Then I casually go and sit in the chair right next to him—no matter how many other empty seats are available. I don't make eye contact or acknowledge him in any way. I just sit there, usually flipping through a magazine, or checking my cell phone for messages.

From my peripheral vision, I can see him getting agitated. He shifts around in his seat, trying to make a little more room between us. Usually he will get up and move. It depends how tightly he holds onto his personal space. Sometimes he shifts his body so his shoulder and part of his back are partially turned toward me, using that part of his body as a barrier.

I've had other people who hold up their newspaper or book to block me out of their personal space.

These are all unconscious reactions to my violation of their personal space. I'm very aware of what they're doing, but they likely are not. Give it a try if you don't mind the awkwardness,

Other, more deliberate reactions to personal space violation include politely asking the person to back up a bit or the more aggressive "back off!" The reaction will depend on how threatened the individual feels, whether they are in a heightened emotional state, and the aggressiveness of their personality.

Mirror, Mirror

Imitation is said to be the sincerest form of flattery. The same concept applies to body language. Mirroring is the action of copying another person's movements and speech. This synchronized communication creates a subconscious bond between the two people. The brain is telling you, "Hey, we're alike!" and your comfort level takes a nice boost.

Mirroring is not intended to copy every single movement. That's annoying and unnerving. Instead, you take on a similar posture, like an open position mirroring the other person's open stance (uncrossed arms and legs). You tilt your head in the same direction, smile if the other person is smiling, and gesture in a similar manner—with the same intensity of movement or lack of it. If your conversational partner leans forward, you do the same. She leans forward and puts her arms on the table and you follow suit.

MIRRORING

MICHAEL'S TIP

When mirroring another person, don't mimic! Follow the pattern of movement. Be similar, not exact. You don't want to get caught mirroring.

Unlike other body language, mirroring also affects your speech. To build rapport with another individual, use a similar tone and pace. If you're naturally a loud and/or fast talker, pay attention to the way the other person is speaking. Adjust your speech to fit.

Language Lab

In this chapter, we talked about personal space, comfort zones, territory, and mirroring. These are essential body language skills that you can sharpen. Here's your homework.

1. When communicating with other people, adjust the space between you to see where the barriers are. Move your chair a little closer or take a step back. Notice the reaction of the other individuals. See how close or far you get before they adjust their own position.

2. Go to a public place, like an airport, shopping mall, or busy downtown street—some place where a lot of strangers are actively moving and stopping. Observe the personal space between them and the reactions. For example, sit in the food court of a mall and watch how people choose and adjust their seats and trays. Look for space violations and reactions. What does that tell you about each person?

3. Practice the subtlety of successful mirroring. In a conversation, adjust your body to reflect the other person's positioning. Note the speech patterns and adjust yours to match.

Liar Liar Pants on Fire!

The body never lies.

—Martha Graham

Little white lies. Fibs. Half-truths. Exaggerations. Falsehoods. Distortion. Misconception. Misinformation. Misinterpretation. Misrepresentation. Misstatement.

Am I missing anything?

There are many words to describe the act of saying something that is not true. And there are even more signals to determine if a person is guilty of it. The body language of liars can betray their deceit to people who are clued into the signs. Whether you're trying to find out who really broke your lamp or whether your employee, colleague, or boss is on the up and up, you need to take the time to learn the non-verbal cues of lying.

The Liar's Rush

When you see something that makes you happy, you smile. When you're cold, you shiver. When you're embarrassed, you blush. When you get excited, you feel your heart race, and your breathing becomes shallower. These are all involuntary reactions triggered by your brain.

And when you lie, your brain shoots messages to different parts of your body. It's natural and easy for your brain to process the truth, but requires much more effort to knowingly tell a lie. Your lying causes internal anxiety and stress, unless you're such a highly practiced deceiver that you either believe your own lies or have learned to manage your responses.

For the average individual, the act of saying something you know to be untrue causes an adrenaline boost. As this hormone streams through the body, the heart rate will increase. On top of that, the muscles tense up, the pupils contract, and the blood pressure and pulse increase. The brain may even cause the liar to break into a sweat. For tobacco users, this rush causes a craving for nicotine, which is why smokers often light up when nervous or stressed.

Polygraph machines rely on the body's natural response to deceitful statements. Let's pretend you are in the hot seat and the machine is hooked up to your body. The sensors will read your pulse, blood pressure, breathing rate, and your perspiration rate. If you have something to hide, it will be a fairly daunting situation. The examiner asks you some simple questions, such as your name and address to get a baseline reading so he can recognize when you're answering truthfully. Then the real questioning begins. They look for spikes in the measurements to indicate which statements may be a lie. If you tell a lie, the polygraph machine is likely to see it—but not 100% of the time. Some people are very good at telling a lie under pressure and can actually fool the machines. They have an ability to stay congruent and as cool as a cucumber.

Remember the episode of Seinfeld when George was training Jerry how to tell a lie? He said, "Jerry, it's not a lie if *you* believe it." It was a funny line, but as far as beating a polygraph, which is what Jerry was about to attempt, it's quite true.

Pathological liars actually believe their stories and are often able to beat the polygraph which is why this isn't a perfect science and not admissible in court, but it's a darn good estimation!

Human Lie Detector

As I mentioned in the introduction, I often play the role of a human lie detector in my corporate presentations. I have 4 volunteers come onto the stage and they are all given a large pad of paper and a marker. I then ask them all to draw some sort of drawing on their pad while my head is turned. The drawing can be of anything the volunteers wish—from a house to a complex technical drawing and everything in between.

The drawings are mixed up and I ask the volunteers to put on their best poker faces. The drawings are then shown to the audience and myself, one at a time. The drawings are usually very funny and amateur looking, which adds to the fun.

The premise of the exercise is for me to try to determine who drew which drawing simply by asking the volunteers some questions. What makes this interesting is that the volunteers are instructed to only answer my questions with the word "no". During the entire exercise I watch their body language for signs of a lie.

Almost every time I guess who drew each of the four drawings. It's not a hard thing to do as their body language changes when they are guilty or under pressure. It may be a big change such as touching their face or it may be a more subtle change such as an eye movement that wasn't natural. I use the same principals on the stage, as I'm about to teach you.

Throughout the exercise I ask the audience if they can determine who drew each drawing as well. Since I just trained them in lie detection, the audience does a darn good job of determining who drew the drawings as well. It's all a hoot!

To Tell the Truth

From head to toe, your body will send out a variety of non-verbal clues when you're being less than honest. Don't rely on one or two signals, but use your body language skills to find enough signs that support the conclusion.

Here are some of the things a liar will do:

✓ **Look up and to the right.** When stating the truth, your brain is recalling, which means it accesses the left side of the brain. The right side controls your creativity, so this is the direction the eyes naturally go when creating a story—in other words, lying.

✓ **Avoid eye contact.** The discomfort (shame, embarrassment, fear of being caught) that underlies lying causes the individual to break eye contact.

✓ **Force eye contact.** Some liars know that avoiding eye contact is a sign of lying, so they go to the extreme and hold your gaze with defiance. You can tell the difference between comfortable eye contact and a staring contest!

✓ **Have contracted pupils.** The pupils get smaller in response to the body's stress level.

✓ **Blink more rapidly.** Increased blinking is a sure sign of nervousness.

✓ **Glance sideways.** The eyes are looking for an escape from an uncomfortable situation.

✓ **Touch the face.** Covering the mouth or rubbing or scratching the nose is a subconscious attempt to cover the face, like hiding the truth

✓ **Nostrils flare.** Flared nostrils can also signal anger, but when combined with other clues on this list, the cue is the faster breathing resulting from dishonesty.

✓ **Force a smile.** A true smile is a natural response. When it's forced, the smile is covering up a meaning other than joy.

✓ **Lick the lips.** The lies are coming from the mouth, which can become dry under stress, causing this direct route to deceit to need a little lubrication.

✓ **Cover the mouth.** This involuntary action subconsciously attempts to block the untruths from emerging.

SOME LIARS MUST TOUCH THEIR MOUTHS OUT OF GUILT. THEY ARE ACTUALLY TOUCHING THE GUILTY BODY PART.

✓ **Swallow repeatedly.** The aforementioned dry mouth can trigger increased swallowing. In some cases, the gesture provides a brief pause to come up with the next part of the lie.

✓ **Sweat.** The increased pulse and heart rate revs up the internal machinery, which causes sweat on the outside.

✓ **Fidget.** Nervous movements, like clicking a pen or tapping fingers, can indicate lying, particularly when combined with other signs.

✓ **Cross the arms quickly.** The closed posture creates a barrier, like defense against being caught in the lie.

✓ **Rubbing hands together.** Muscles tense as a result of the stress of creating or telling falsehoods. Rubbing the hands together is a self-soothing response to the tightening of the muscles.

BE AWARE OF THIS SELF-SOOTHING GESTURE.

✓ **Clench fists.** A more extreme response to the tensing muscles, the clenched fists can indicate anger or lying, so be sure to pay attention to other cues.

✓ **Hide hands.** Tucking hands into pockets, behind your back or anywhere out of sight reflects a secretive behavior—consciously or unconsciously. Whether hiding something in your closed palms or keeping the truth in your head, the hands are a good clue to honesty.

✓ **Speak with palms facing downward.** The upward palm is a sign of trust showing that there's nothing hidden. When the palms are averted, it's reasonable to suspect a cover-up.

✓ **Wipe hands.** Palms can get sweaty when a person is nervous or lying. Look for someone who is wiping away the moisture at an abnormal rate.

✓ **Cross the legs suddenly.** Just as with the arms, suddenly crossed legs form a self-protecting barrier. Whether sitting or standing, if the person quickly sets up this obstacle, then there's something being hidden behind it.

✓ **Tuck feet.** Hiding any part of the body indicates the person is holding something back. If the feet are tucked under a chair when seated, it's like shoving hands in pockets to protect the truth from being discovered.

✓ **Stiffen posture.** With all that muscle-tightening going on, the body takes on an overall tense posture. Arms are pulled into the sides and the individual appears unusually rigid.

✓ **Move away.** A person who is lying doesn't like to face you directly. They might avert their gaze, but you should also look at the body position. Is he standing to the side or at an angle? If so, he literally can't face up to the truth.

Verbal Cues

Although body language forms meanings from non-verbal movements, there are clues that are not quite non-verbal, but still need to be recognized, particularly when it comes to identifying a liar. For example, the truth is much easier to share than a lie, which requires creative construction. When you ask a question, for example, the liar takes a bit longer to respond and will speak more slowly. The tone might be more controlled as the lie takes shape and the pitch might go higher.

Remember that a person's normal body language varies from one individual to another. Some people are just antsier or more distracted than others. A fidgeter could just be bored or restless, not dishonest. And someone who sweats a lot could have medical issues. Make sure you consider all the factors before you shout out, "Liar, liar, pants on fire!"

Look Over Here!

Richard Bandler and John Grinder are the founders of Neuro-linguistic programming (NLP). If you know nothing bout NLP, do yourself a huge favor and dive into it. You'll learn how to program your own brain to create change in yourself... and in others. Bandler and Grinder conducted extensive studies to understand how the eyes reflect the brain's activity. We touched on eye-movements in Chapter 4, but here we dive in a little deeper. In their groundbreaking book "Frogs Into Princes: The Introduction to Neuro-Linguistic Programming", Bandler and Grinder created six different "visual accessing clues":

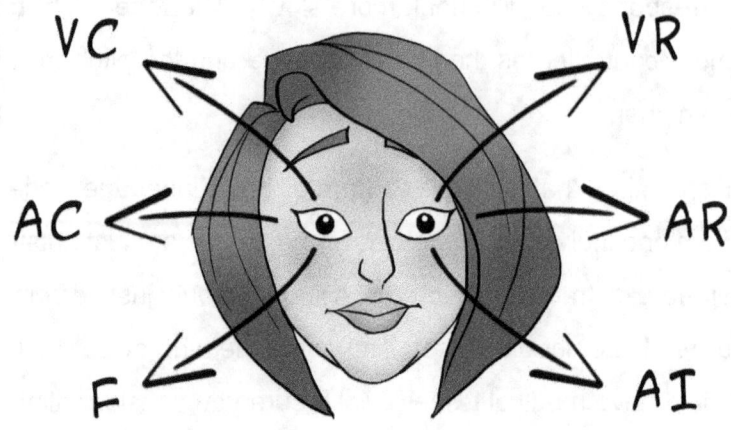

COMPLETE NLP EYE ACCESSING ILLUSTRATION

Each of these eye positions is based on your perspective, looking directly at the other person.

UP AND TO THE PERSONS RIGHT =
VISUALLY CONSTRUCTING (VC)

When a person looks up and to their right this means they are seeing something in their minds eye that they are constructing or creating. In order to access this part of the brain that gives us these constructed images, we must (if only for a fraction of a second) use our eyes to receive the image.

UP AND TO THE LEFT =
VISUALLY REMEMBERED OR RECALLED (VR)

When a person looks up and to the right, they are seeing a picture of something they remember. For example, if you ask a person what they ate for breakfast they will need to look up and to the left in order to see the previously eaten scrambled eggs and bacon.

How are the two previous eye-accessing cues especially helpful when it comes to becoming a human lie detector?

Imagine this...

You have a sneaky suspicion that your son wasn't attending the high school football game last night. Oh, he says he was there, but you are suspicious of a lie. You then become an interrogator and ask the following.

"Who were you with last night?" He looks up and to the left (visually remembering) and says, *"I was with Rich and Stephen."* You are setting him up for the real question in a moment. You are asking the simple questions first and creating a baseline just like a polygraph test.

"Where did you eat?" (which is another question where the answer can easily be visualized) Again, he looks up and to the left. *"We ate at Taco Bell."*

"Who else did you see at the game?" There's the zinger! You want to see if he is going to "remember" his answer on the left or "construct" it on the right.

He looks up and to the right (visually creating/constructing) and says, "I saw Paul, Alex, Britney, Sean, and Katie."

You make an accurate assumption that your son didn't see any of these people at the game, since he had to construct those names from the creative side of his brain. You then move from interrogator to judge and jury.

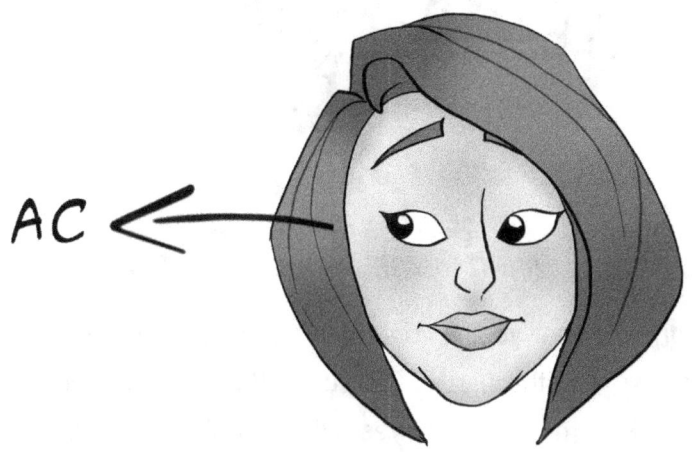

DIRECTLY TO THE RIGHT =
AUDITORY CONSTRUCTED (AC).

This is another creative thought, but involves imagining a sound, rather than an image. For example, "Imagine the sound of dropping a marble into a metal bucket. In order to create this sound we must go directly to the right to construct it.

**DIRECTLY TO THE LEFT =
AUDITORY REMEMBERED (AR).**

Can you hear your favorite song in your head? If you can, you went to the part of your brain that recalls sounds and you likely moved your eyes either slightly or directly to the left. Our eyes go there anytime we remember a sound or are remembering what somebody may have said to us.

**DOWN AND TO THE RIGHT =
FEELING / KINESTHETIC (F).**

This movement reflects recalling a sensory experience, like a feeling or a touch. "Do you remember the smell of fresh baked bread or the feeling of the sun on your face?"

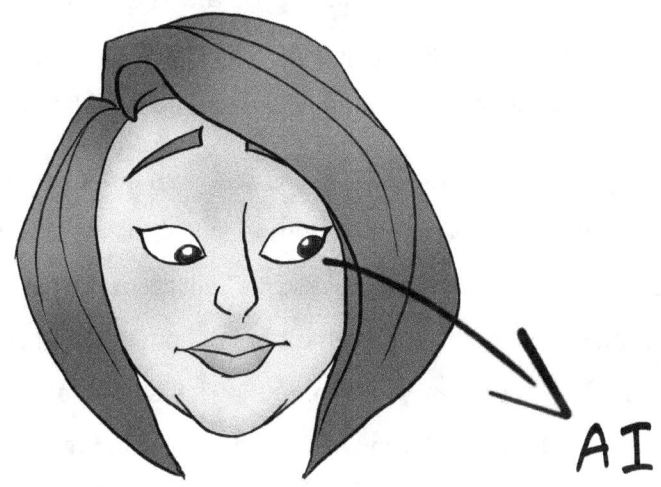

AI

DOWN AND TO THE LEFT = AUDIO INTERNAL (AI).

When you're having a discussion with yourself, your eyes show that there's a conversation going on. Look around, if you see someone looking down and to the left they are likely in more than just deep thought. They may be reasoning, discussing, and negotiating with themselves.

As a speaker, I use these eye-accessing cues from the platform for feedback. I also use them in day-to-day life to see what may be going through someone's head. Want to blow someone's mind? Next time you are at a store and the cashier is looking up and to the left, ask him/her what picture they just saw in their head. It's always good for a laugh.

But it goes further than just laughs. You can use these eye-accessing cues to know if a person is visualizing, hearing sounds, in touch with their feeling, or talking to themselves. You can even tell if they are remember or constructing. When you put it all together, you can gain a real sense for what's going on in their mind and *you* become the mind reader.

Let's Throw in Some Confusion... Not Really

These eye-accessing cues are simple enough to remember, but one thing must be kept in mind. If a person is left-handed, everything get's reversed. Which means recall/remember goes to the right and create/construct goes to the left. You can even go ahead and swap AI (audio internal) and F (feeling or kinesthetic).

Why is this? Simply put, the brains of left-handed people are a mirror image of right-handers, so everything gets turned on its head.

Want to know if someone is a lefty or a righty? What wrist is their watch on? What hand do they eat with? Which had holds their cell phone? Lefties make up for about 10% of the population.

May I Have Your Attention? Smart Moves for Presenters

> Language is a more recent technology. Your body language, your eyes, your energy will come through to your audience before you even start speaking.
>
> —Peter Guber

Have you ever sat in an audience and watched a presenter stand stiffly, squirm, sweat, and make all sorts of uncomfortable gestures? And did you feel equally uncomfortable watching this spectacle?

Conversely, think about the times when a presenter stood in front of a group, confident and in control. She makes eye contact with people in the audience. She moves easily across the stage or around the room. Her body language makes you feel at ease, and in turn, you have increased focus on what she's saying. Her credibility quotient soared, right?

You can have a wealth of knowledge, invaluable insights, and important news to deliver, but if your body language doesn't support you with confident posture and "tells", then you might as well take a seat and let someone else deliver your presentation.

"Food Network Star" is a television show that pits culinary folks of different backgrounds against each other to compete for their own cooking show on this network. Every week, they have the contestants make an on-camera presentation to see how they perform in front of an audience. One week, they gave meters to the audience members to gauge their opinion of the presenters. Each person could move the dial up and down in order to communicate their approval or disapproval of what they witnessed. One by one, the contestants did their sixty-second presentations. A few of them were extremely entertaining and confident, and they scored well throughout their minute of fame. Others made awkward movements or statements and stumbled through their pitch. The audience was clearly uncomfortable and unimpressed, which they demonstrated by cranking their meters down low.

Remember that only about seven percent of your message is communicated through what you say, so you must invest in sharpening your body talk before stepping in front of a group.

You probably won't have an audience of people armed with approval meters, but you should perform as though you did. In this chapter, I will cover key body talk tactics to help you boost your presentation power.

Take Ownership

When an audience gathers to hear what you have to say, these people want you to inspire, motivate, and educate them. They expect you to be powerful, entertaining, engaging, and influential. In other words, they want you to "own" them. Of course, you have to present a compelling message with your words and images, but the way you use your body language will either support that result or whittle away at every single point, until they no longer hear your words but focus solely on your gestures.

Follow these eight tips for building a connection with the people you're trying to influence.

1
Get casual

If you're wearing a suit jacket, unbutton it. When your clothing is all buttoned up, so are you. Get comfortable. Relax.

2
Stand comfortably

Use your stance to show that you welcome the group, are open to them, and feel confident and relaxed in their presence. Stand with your feet pointing toward them when you're addressing the group. Your feet should be about a shoulder's distance apart—not together, which is a rigid, closed posture—so your weight is balanced and you look at ease.

3
Point with two fingers, not one

A single finger pointing at an individual comes across as accusatory. When you're trying to emphasize a point, use your index and middle finger together—and wave them rather than jab.

4
Look at your audience, not your notes

Whether you have a stack of note cards on a podium or in your hand, or a teleprompter feeding you a script, don't be a slave to those aids. Anyone can get up and read. Your audience wants to know that your presentation comes from your own knowledge, and when your eyes dart back and forth between them and your notes, you disconnect from the group. Be prepared enough that you don't need to constantly refer to your prompts.

5
Relax your posture, but don't slouch

Crossed arms may signal a defensive posture, that you're protecting yourself or covering up. Putting your hands in your pockets also conveys that you're hiding something. Relax. Keep your arms comfortably at your sides when you're not gesturing. But remember to stand straight, a sure sign of confidence!

6
Make eye contact with audience members

When you look another person in the eye, you communicate honesty, interest, and authenticity. Sure, it's tougher when you're working a crowd, but you can pick out individuals as you walk around the room or the stage, and make eye contact with them, rather than continually scanning the crowd, or staring at your notes.

7
Move

It's more natural to move around as you speak to a group. If you walk casually about—not pacing—you can address different parts of your audience and keep them engaged. Standing in one place will cause your listeners' interest to wane because it's harder (and more boring) to maintain focus on a stationery object.

8
Gesture gently

Use your hands to emphasize your statements, but keep your motions simple and subtle. Broad, sweeping arm movements distract your audience. More subtle hand gestures of your hands, arms, and head will enhance what you're saying. Nodding, smiling, opening your hands with palms facing out or up, and steepling your fingers are positive gestures to incorporate into your presentation.

A CONFIDENT PRESENTER WILL SMILE, GESTURE,
MAKE EYE CONTACT, AND ISN'T AFRAID TO MOVE.

A NERVOUS SPEAKER WILL SLOUCH, PERSPIRE, LOOK AWAY, AND GIVE SELF-SOOTHING GESTURES

The Dubious Listener

The whole reason you're standing in front of a group is to influence them. Maybe you're trying to teach them something new, which means they must have confidence in your credibility. Or you might be trying to encourage them to purchase something as a result of your presentation, so they need to feel that you are honest and reliable.

It would be great if question marks appeared over the heads of people who weren't quite convinced, so you could turn your attention toward converting them. In the absence of that clue, try looking for these signs that your listeners aren't buying into you or your message:

1

Chin stroking

This is an evaluation gesture. It means they're considering what you're saying, but not yet certain.

2

Crossed arms

A defensive gesture, the crossed arms create a barrier between the listener and the speaker that says, "keep away!"

3

Body turned away

A person who is engaged in a conversation—whether listening or speaking—faces in the direction of the speaker or listener. If members of your audience are turned away from you, even slightly, they are protecting themselves from your frontal assault.

4

Rubbing the eyes, neck, or face

Rubbing a hand over any of the areas around the head or face signifies consideration. The person is pondering what you are saying, but not yet agreeing with or accepting it.

5

Defensive crossed-leg position

The legs are crossed so that one ankle rests on the opposite knee. This is sometimes called a "figure four" posture because the leg position (sort of) looks like the number four. What the leg crosser may be doing here is creating a barricade that communicates, "You're not getting through here."

6

Lack of eye contact

People who are honest, confident, and engaged in a conversation make eye contact. When a listener averts her eyes, she is shielding the truth that she has doubts about you or your presentation.

IS YOUR AUDIENCE ENGAGED?

You're Losing Them

While your audience is reading your body language, be sure you're tuned into theirs. Pay attention to their interest level. Here are some cues that will signal that their focus is shifting from interest and belief to boredom or doubt.

1
Not sitting upright

Slouching in a seat is a sign that the person is disengaging from your presentation, or the chair is uncomfortable. Either way, they're not paying attention to you, so be sure to look for those people who are literally slipping away from you.

2
Fidgeting

When you notice people squirming, shifting in their seats, crossing and uncrossing their legs, or any other fidgeting motions, you have a restless audience that is not focusing on you the way you'd like.

3
Looking at something or someone other than you

Any time attention is diverted away from you—checking for texts or emails, reading, talking to another person, adjusting clothing, rummaging through a bag, or obsessing over a speck of lint—it's a sure sign that you're not effectively communicating.

4
Jiggling foot

You've seen it. Maybe you've even done it yourself. The fast, foot bouncing is a sign of anxiousness. When you see this in an audience member, you have a person who doesn't want to be there at that moment.

5
Making exit signs

They're looking at their watches, or eyeing the door. Maybe they're sitting on the edge of the seat like a kid ready to bolt out of class when the bell rings. When a listener has one foot out the door, they might as well be gone altogether, because you've lost their attention.

6
Resting head

Bored or daydreaming, the person with the head resting on a hand, the back of the seat, or propped up by some other method is having trouble paying attention.

7
Yawning

Yawning results from fatigue, boredom, or lack of oxygen and all of these situations mean an audience member is fading away from your gripping presentation. The worst part about yawning is the infectious nature. You see a person yawning in the audience and you might mirror the action, prompting your other listeners to think *you're* disinterested.

MICHAEL'S TIP

Be sure to have strong, open, confident body language for 10 minutes before your presentation. Then carry it to the stage and your audience will know you own the room.

Group dynamics are a tough thing. Bear in mind that people come to a presentation with their own agendas and issues. Some people may be terribly distracted even before they sit down. Others have emergencies that come up. It's normal to have some audience members not paying attention, but when you see a wide range of body language in the group that tells you they're not interested, then you need to adjust your presentation. Take a break. Encourage them to stand up and stretch while you regroup. Make a sudden movement to grab their attention. Change the tone of your voice. Walk around, closer to them. Ask questions of individuals to wake them up. And make sure your body is speaking with the same high energy.

Language Lab

Addressing a group of people requires a conversational level of body language fluency. You need to control your own body talk while also reading that of your audience so that you maintain their interest and exert the influence you desire.

Here are some exercises to sharpen those skills.

1. Watch online videos of motivational speakers both living and passed, such as Zig Ziglar, Tony Robbins, Les Brown, Ronald Reagan, and Martin Luther King What body language traits do you see? How do they impact you?

2. Check out some infomercials or home shopping programs. What body language cues do the spokespeople use? Do they come across as sincere?

3. The next time you attend a group presentation, notice the body language cues of the presenter and the audience. What do you see? What can you learn from their signals?

4. Practice doing a presentation in front of a mirror. Focus more on your body language than on your speech. Try incorporating the gestures outlined here in this chapter. Can you see the difference it makes?

Best Foot Forward— The Interview

A blur of blinks, taps, jiggles, pivots and shifts... the body language of a man wishing urgently to be elsewhere.

—Edward R. Murrow

Do you remember your last job interview? How'd it go? Did you walk out of there thinking you nailed it, or were you riddled with doubt?

Since 55 percent of communication is non-verbal, what was your body saying while your mouth was talking? And were your motions and gestures drowning out your words?

In the last chapter, I offered tips for using body language to make a more compelling presentation. When you're in an interview, however, you face a more intimate situation than presenting yourself to a group. Even if several people are interviewing you simultaneously, you are physically closer and more involved in a dialogue (versus a monologue)—which means your body language is critical.

Let's go through the body language techniques that will present the positive impression you're striving for.

First Look

Your first impression doesn't start with the greeting. Your interviewer is sizing you up visually before you say a word. Each moment leading up to the meeting—when you step out of your car in the parking lot, enter the building, wait for a visitor's pass, ride the elevator—you are being seen by someone, perhaps even your interviewer. Be aware of your body language every step of the way! Gestures like rubbing your neck, darting glances everywhere, nervously tapping your foot, or clutching too tightly to your briefcase bring attention to your discomfort.

When you're sitting and waiting, what are you doing? Are you relaxed (or at least pretending to be) or fidgeting—crossing and uncrossing your legs, squirming in the chair, with your eyes darting around the room?

While you're waiting to be interviewed, sit up straight with good (but not rigid) posture. Keep your feet planted on the floor. Your legs shouldn't be "splayed" out in front of you, because that communicates too much comfort, lack of energy, and carelessness. You can cross your legs, but don't jiggle them or repeatedly cross and uncross them.

Keep your hands on your lap. Don't fidget with an item in your hand or clutch your bag, tablet, or other paraphernalia with a white-knuckle hold.

Try to position yourself so that you're facing in the direction where the interviewer will enter so you can make a "head on" presentation. Avoid having multiple items on your lap that you'll have to shuffle quickly in order to stand up and greet that person.

WAIT PATIENTLY AND PROFESSIONALLY.
YOU NEVER KNOW WHO'S WATCHING.

The Handshake

In Chapter 2, I covered the various types of handshakes and what they communicate. Before heading to your interview, take a few minutes to refresh yourself on the different handshakes and their meanings. Not only do you want to communicate the right one, but it will be interesting for you to understand what the other person is "saying" with their choice of shake.

I know you might be nervous about the interview, so if your palm is sweating, be sure to wipe your hand before offering it. Be sure to be discrete about this step, because, as you've heard before, "never let them see you sweat!"

Remember that you're not trying to overpower your interviewer, so don't deliver a death grip. A firm grasp is good, but don't overdo it. And keep it short—one pump or two is plenty.

You can show respect by extending your hand with your palm turned slightly upward. There's a subtle message here when the interviewer's hand rests on top of your own. It says you are there to serve and you know the boss is in charge.

Keep to the one-handed shake. If you reach out and cover the interviewer's hand with your own, you're showing a false sense of friendship that hasn't been established at this point in the relationship with the interviewer.

NEVER BE AGGRESSIVE.
LET YOUR POTENTIAL BOSS LEAD YOU.

Posture and Position

Your interviewer might indicate where you should sit, but if not, wait to see where he or she sits down and be sure you are facing directly across. Don't sit with your body turned at an angle from the interviewer or leaning backward, because you'll come across as disengaged.

If you have a table or desk between the two of you, avoid the temptation to pile your personal belongings there. Don't create a barrier with your "stuff". If you have a portfolio, computer bag, handbag, computer, tablet, or other items, put them on the floor next to your feet. You also don't want to look like you're moving in.

Sit up straight to show alertness and interest. Slouching demonstrates laziness and lack of self-confidence. Sit squarely on the chair, not on the edge, which shows the unspoken desire to escape. Lean forward only slightly, to communicate interest without invading personal space. If the other person leans back, it could be a sign that you're too close.

Your sitting position should communicate that you're confident and comfortable. Keep your hands on your lap or folded on the table. Your feet should be on the floor neatly. Any crossing of limbs presents a closed, potentially defensive posture.

While you're seated, try to maintain your good posture. Avoid rocking back and forth, or repositioning yourself in your chair. You'll appear nervous, uncomfortable, and unfocused.

Eyes and Face

It's all about eye contact—in the right amount and intensity. Look at your interviewer to show your interest, but don't stare. Hold eye contact for about ten seconds, look briefly away, and then regain the visual hold—without the darting glances all over the place that indicate you are unnerved. If you notice your interviewer looking in another direction, he or she might be trying to follow your own gaze, so watch for the signs that your eyes are giving you away.

Now, let's say your interviewer is interrupted—maybe taking an important phone call or someone pokes their head in with the inevitable "quick question". What do you do? Don't stare. Divert your glance during the unexpected break—a sign that you're not intruding; even though it's obvious you can hear what's going on. You should turn your gaze sideways, not down, because it can seem disinterested or insincere (unless you're reading something). However, don't take the opportunity to check your phone for messages or get out of your seat and walk around. These responses would create a much bigger distraction than the interviewer's interlude,

If more than one person is interviewing you, be sure to make eye contact periodically with each one. Address your responses to more than one individual to keep them all engaged in what you're saying, while always returning to the person who is speaking to you.

MICHAEL'S TIP

Size up your interviewer. Is he/she happy? Anxious? Bored? Pleased with you? When you have some information, use it to your advantage so the interview falls in your favor. Remember mirroring? Mirror your interviewer.

I remember a woman being interviewed who was obsessed with lint on her skirt. Rather than focus on the discussion, her eyes kept darting down and she picked away at this unseen fleck. The interviewer was both distracted and annoyed, because this woman was unfocused on the important discussion.

Another interviewee told me he couldn't help but stare at a rather large blemish on his interviewer's face. I told him she probably was well aware of it and even self-conscious, and that he wasn't winning any extra points by bringing attention to her "pain point".

The lesson here: Focus on the eyes of your interviewer, not the lint on your clothes, a stain, a distraction, or any other kind of oddity.

Smile and nod in moderation. You don't want to look like a Bobblehead, mindlessly bouncing on the dashboard.

Avoid rubbing your neck or face or tugging your ear. You'll appear dubious or deceitful.

SHAKE YOUR HEAD IN AGREEMENT
BUT DON'T BE A BOBBLEHEAD.

Hands and Arms

Nerves move through your body and out to your extremities—hands and feet. Then they stop there. But your nervousness and excitement doesn't. This is why people shuffle their feet around, drum their fingers, jiggle their feet, or try to figure out what to do with their hands when their nerves are over-stimulated. By being aware of the issue, you can focus your body language to communicate the message of a calm, assured person, even when your insides are screaming otherwise.

Your arms should remain uncrossed and at your side. Don't fold them across your chest, because you create a barrier that could be taken as defensive, resistant or superior. Putting your arms and hands behind your head is too relaxed, and comes across as cocky.

Use your hands to reinforce your message, not shout over it. Avoid sweeping, or jerky gestures; they should be subtle, so your movements won't distract the listener. Instead, keep your hands folded when listening. When you speak, position your hands openly, with palms up, to convey honesty and sincerity.

Image consultant Alison Craig, author of "Hello Job! How to Psych Up, Suit Up & Show Up", says you should keep your hands in the space above the table and below your collarbone. "Any higher and you're going to appear frantic," she says.

The last two tips I want to offer here reflect common manners. Remember what your parents (or grandparents) taught you: It's rude to point. If you need to direct the listener to something, use the two-finger point (index and middle finger), again, with your palm either sideways or pointing upward. A palm facing down represents a closed posture, like you're hiding something; open means sincere and honest.

Finally, another Mom-ism: No elbows on the table! Well, at least, don't use your elbows to prop up your hands so you can rest your face on them. This could be interpreted as boredom.

Feet and Legs

All those nerve endings are gathered in your feet, a dead end for your nervous energy. So you jiggle your foot, cross and uncross your legs and ankles, and tap your toes. You might not even realize you're doing it.

But your interviewer does.

Tame the nervous energy happening down below. Keep your feet planted on the floor or cross your legs at your ankles. And keep them there during the interview. The more you shuffle about, the more you distract your interviewer. And the movements convey your anxiety.

Michael C. Anthony

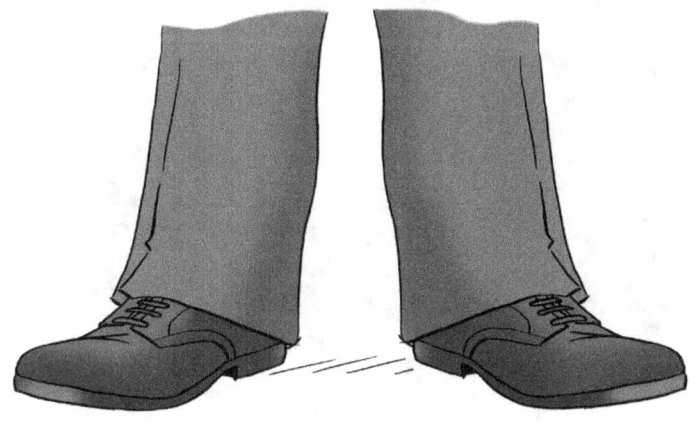

FEET UNDER THE TABLE – THIS IS GOOD

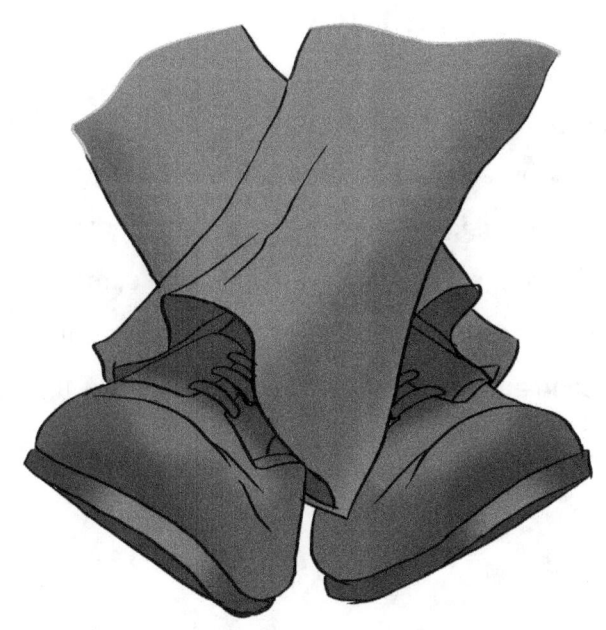

FEET UNDER THE TABLE – THIS IS ACCEPTABLE,
BUT DON'T GET TOO COMFORTABLE.

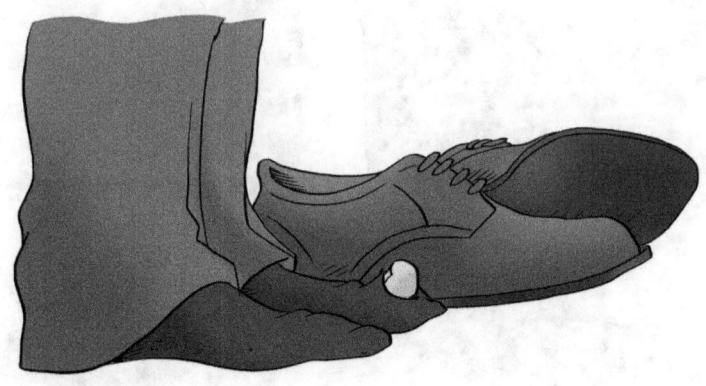

FEET UNDER THE TABLE - UHHHH - NO.

Parting Ways

Everything positive that has happened in your interview can be marred by a bad exit. Before you get up, gather your personal belongings. Doing it after can appear disorganized. Then stand up, smile politely, and offer the same firm, brief handshake (palm turned slightly upward) as you did on your introduction and let the interviewer guide you out. If you take the lead, you're showing dominance.

Language Lab

With so much riding on the messages you communicate in an interview, be sure your body language is fluent. Take the time to perfect your body language before your interview.

1. Practice in front of a mirror. Place a chair and table in front of a mirror large enough to see yourself, head to toe. Work on each area of your body language: posture, face, eyes, hands, arms, legs, and feet. Find the position that looks comfortable, attentive, and professional. Then put it all together and work on holding that complete position. Whenever you sit down at your kitchen table or desk, assume that position to build your muscle memory, which makes it easier for the "pose" to become automatic.

2. Work on your gesturing. Watch yourself in the mirror as you use your hands in various ways: folded, steepled fingers, pointing, etc.

3. Practice your facial expressions, such as interest, curiosity, agreement, and sincerity.

4. "Rehearse" all of this body language with a friend who can give you an honest opinion on the messages you're conveying. Try different movements, postures, and expressions, and then ask, "What does this 'say' to you?"

Working It Out: Body Talk with Bosses, Employees, Colleagues, and Clients

> Actions speak louder than words, but not nearly as often.

—Mark Twain

By this point, you've developed a conversational grasp of body language. In this chapter, I want to interpret some of the non-verbal cues that are common in business interactions. Whether you're dealing with a co-worker, or your boss, trying to build confidence in a client, or determine whether someone in the office is flirting with you, having a better knowledge of body language is a real job skill.

So, here's your quick guide to navigating office interactions.

Please note that I didn't include the obvious clues, like smiling, frowning, or running in the opposite direction when you appear. And we've already covered handshakes, so I'm not going to repeat those signs.

Sizing Up Your Boss

It's your boss's job to inspire, motivate, and coach you to achieve your best performance.

In a perfect world, you'd have that supervisor—the person who tells you when you're doing great and offers constructive criticism to help you grow. But until you have that dream job, take the time to understand how to use body language with the person in charge.

"I'm not happy"

✓ Lack of eye contact

✓ Arms folded

✓ Fists clenched

✓ Furrowed brow

✓ Pursed lips

✓ Pacing

✓ Tugging at shirt collar

✓ Feet are together when standing (closed stance)

✓ Hands on hips and leaning forward (even slightly)

✓ Leaning against a wall while speaking

✓ Arms behind back, with one hand gripping the other arm (self-control)

✓ Standing with legs crossed

"I don't agree", "I doubt it" or "frustration."

✓ Rubbing eyes

✓ Pinching nose, head down with eyes closed

✓ Rubbing the back of the neck

✓ Peering over the top of the eyeglasses

✓ Touching the nose

✓ Picking at lint

✓ Squinting

WE'VE ALL FELT LIKE THIS BEFORE.

"You're doing a good/great job!"

✓ Speaking with palms up

✓ Patting you on the shoulder or back

✓ Eye contact

✓ Comfortable seated posture in your presence—sitting back with arms to the side (uncrossed)

✓ Open stance when standing

MICHAEL'S TIP

Remember, the boss is always right—even when he's not. If you challenge, tread those waters carefully

Reading Your Workers

Are you beloved by your employees—or just kidding yourself? Look for the following signs to clue you into their unspoken wishes.

"Yeah, yeah, yeah. Can you stop talking now?"

✓ Body or feet are facing away from you

✓ Lack of eye contact

✓ Shifting weight from one foot to the other

✓ Squirming in a chair

✓ Jiggling foot

✓ Tapping finger

✓ Fidgeting with an object, like a pen, keys or cell phone

✓ Frequent blinking

✓ Rummaging through desk or bag

✓ Looking at phone or computer screen

"You're making me uncomfortable."

✓ Tugging at the shirt collar

✓ Darting eyes

✓ Moves away (expanding personal space)

✓ Biting corner of lip

✓ Crossing and uncrossing legs

✓ Touching or adjusting clothing

✓ Ankles crossed (fighting the desire to flee)

✓ Clutching items to chest, like folders, books, laptop (creating barrier)

"Can I interrupt here?"

✓ Slightly moving hand upward (seeking recognition)

✓ Touching or tapping lips with index finger (holding back words)

✓ Tugging earlobe

"I'm happy!"

✓ Sitting back in chair when listening (comfortable)

✓ Leaning slightly forward in conversation (engaged)

✓ Hand on chest when expressing satisfaction (sincerity)

✓ Good eye contact

✓ Body and feet are pointed in your direction when talking

✓ Arms and legs are uncrossed (relaxed and open)

✓ Feet are apart when standing (open stance)

CAN YOU READ THEIR MINDS
BY READING THEIR BODIES?

Is Your Customer Always Right?

Building a good relationship with a client requires strong communication, both verbal and non-verbal. Remember that it's always more cost-effective to maintain an existing client than to search for new ones, so it pays to understand what they're **not** saying out loud. To create the atmosphere of trust—in your knowledge, choices and ethics—pay attention to these clues.

"I'm not sure you're on the right track."

✓ Rubbing the face or back of the neck

✓ Pinching nose with eyes closed

- ✓ Clenched hands
- ✓ Peering over the top of the eyeglasses
- ✓ Touching the nose
- ✓ Picking at lint
- ✓ Squinting
- ✓ Hand on the cheek with the index finger pointing up

"I like what you have to say."

- ✓ Leaning forward slightly while listening
- ✓ Arms and legs are not crossed (open posture)
- ✓ Body and feet are turned toward you
- ✓ Good eye contact
- ✓ Stroking the chin
- ✓ Open stance with hands on hips
- ✓ Unclasped hands with palms up
- ✓ Nodding

"I've got the upper hand here."

✓ Steepled fingers

✓ Sitting back

✓ Hands behind the head

✓ Leg crossed with one ankle over opposite knee

✓ Hands in pocket with thumbs out

✓ Touching or grasping jacket lapel with thumb pointing up

✓ Standing with hands clasped behind the back

The Office Flirt

The body language of flirtation was a whole lot easier when we were kids. If a girl shoved a boy, or was aggressive in any way, she probably liked him. Conversely, a boy would totally ignore a girl he liked.

Flirting is a means of checking out the attraction level. It happens all the time in the workplace where there is so much social interaction throughout the day. But how can you tell the difference between friendly conversation and flirtation? Well, there are some distinct signs. Men and women often flirt in different ways, but some clues are unisex.

Women

✓ Flicking the hair

✓ Preening (smoothing or adjusting clothes, hair, or make-up)

✓ Smile with head tilt

✓ Wetting lips

✓ Fingernail between teeth

✓ Frequently sipping a drink

✓ Touching sensitive areas like wrist and front of the neck

✓ Stroking hair

✓ Leaning on hand or fist with wrist pointing at you

✓ Playing with jewelry

✓ Dilated pupils

✓ Steady eye contact

✓ Batting eyelashes

✓ Laughs easily (not forced)

✓ Close space (less than two feet from you)

✓ Good posture

✓ Stroking objects, like wine glass stem or pen

✓ Good posture

✓ Incidental body contact, particularly if it recurs

Men

✓ Flared nostrils

✓ Puffed-up chest

✓ Hands on his hips

✓ Hands in pockets with thumbs out

✓ Preening (adjusting clothes or hair)

✓ Frequently sipping a drink

✓ Stroking hair

✓ Leaning on hand or fist with wrist pointing toward you

✓ Playing with jewelry

✓ Dilated pupils

✓ Steady eye contact

✓ Laughs easily (not forced)

✓ Close space (less than two feet from you)

- ✓ Compares a woman's size—e.g., hands, feet, height—to his, showing that he is interested in the details

- ✓ Good posture

- ✓ Incidental body contact, particularly if it recurs

"GET A ROOM!"

Language Lab

You probably spend a majority of your time on the job, interacting with a wide variety of people—some who you like and others you need to respect or, at least, tolerate. You can sharpen you body language skills in common work situations with these exercises.

1. Watch the interactions between people in your office and try to interpret the meaning. Later, share your observations with them. For example, "You seemed to be a little uncomfortable after the meeting. Is that right?" Or "You looked like you got some well-deserved praise. Did you?"

2. Watch an episode of a show that takes place at work—such as "The Office", "Entourage", "Parks and Recreation", or "Mad Men"—with the sound muted. What do you see in the body language of the actors?

3. Role-play the various situations described in this chapter. Give the non-verbal clues to someone you know, without letting them know the meaning. Ask the other person for feedback on what your body language communicated.

Translation, Please! Multicultural Body Talk

> Americans who travel abroad for the first time are often shocked to discover that, despite all the progress that has been made in the last 30 years, many foreign people still speak in foreign languages.
>
> —Dave Barry

America has become a multicultural melting pot. The foreign-born population in this country increased from 8.8 million in 2000 to more than 40 million in 2010, according to the U.S. Census.

And while many of our "New Americans" are learning the English language, they still have inherent cultural differences that affect communication with native-born Americans. Many of the gestures that we take for granted as acceptable in our culture are offensive to people from other countries.

Whether you work with or for New Americans, or are pursuing them as clients or employees, you need to understand that something as simple as a "thumbs up" sign, or handshake could send the wrong message.

So, let's look at American body language as it is translated around the world.

Face It—We See Things Differently

In any conversation, your face says more than your words. Pay attention to what you're communicating with facial expressions and movements to someone who wasn't born and raised in our culture.

Smiling. We think we're being pleasant when we smile at someone, but to some Japanese and Korean people, you may appear mindless.

Nodding. In America, a nod signifies agreement. In Asian countries, like Japan, they may simply be trying to tell you they are listening. Don't assume it's a "yes"!

Raising eyebrows. Don't automatically take raised eyebrows as a sign of surprise or doubt. Filipino natives use the raised eyebrows as a way of saying "hello".

Tugging the ear. In East Indian culture, the ear is a sacred appendage. If you pull, scratch or rub it, you indicate you have done something wrong and are seeking to repent.

Tapping the nose. British people see this gesture as a sign that you're sharing a secret, or hiding something.

Sucking the thumb. When someone from The Netherlands puts the tip of his thumb in his mouth, don't expect him to curl up in the fetal position, but you should be concerned, because he's showing he doesn't believe you.

Look out!

Our eyes communicate so much. We need to be aware that people who are not native to our culture may interpret certain movements differently.

Eye contact. Throughout this book, I have told you that good eye contact is a sign of honesty and interest. Well, my caveat is—not with everyone! Some people in the following cultures believe looking another person in the eye is disrespectful:

✓ Asian

✓ Latin American

✓ Caribbean

✓ African

Conversely, Middle Easterners and many European people believe strong eye contact—even more intense than we might be comfortable with—represents honesty. If you look away, they may become distrustful of you.

Closing eyes. When speaking to Asians—specifically Thai, Chinese and Japanese—you might see them close their eyes. Don't worry. You haven't offended them, or put them to sleep. They are indicating that they are listening and considering what you have said. Their closed eyes are the same as a nod, so they're signifying an affirmative— "I agree" or "Yes".

MICHAEL'S TIP

If you are travelling overseas or doing business with someone that has travelled to see you, do your research first. Many opportunities have been lost because of innocent ignorance.

Handy Help

From the subtle movement of one finger to the wave of your hand, you send out a lot of information. But is your desired message being received? Check out these differences.

Winking. You might think you're sending a friendly sign with your wink, but many Taiwanese, East Indians, and Australians will be offended.

BE CAREFUL,
A FRIENDLY WINK CAN BE TAKEN THE WRONG WAY.

Shaking hands. It's normal for Americans to extend a hand in greeting and, while many other countries recognize this practice, it may not be the best way to welcome them. Asians prefer a bow, as they are hesitant about physical contact. Indian and Saudi women do not want to be touched by a stranger. To be safe, wait for the other person to extend a hand first.

Finger pointing. East Indian, Asian, and Middle Eastern cultures are offended by pointing with one finger. Some British are similarly offended. If you need to indicate something, point with two fingers or with all your fingers.

If you ask for directions at a Disney Resort or at The Apple Store, you'll notice the employee will point with two fingers instead of one.

POINTING WITH TWO FINGERS INSTEAD OF ONE IS BECOMING UNIVERSAL.

Crooking the finger. Japanese people consider the "come here" gesture of beckoning someone with your crooked finger an obscene gesture. In some Southeast Asian countries, this motion is considered as a threatening gesture when waved at a child or as just, plain rude when used on an adult. People in Yugoslavia, Malaysia, and Vietnam use the same gesture to call animals, so they will definitely be offended if you direct them in this way.

Flashing the "OK" sign. Making a circle with your thumb and forefinger may be "A-OK" in the United States, but Russians and Brazilians equate that to flipping the middle finger.

WHAT WE ASSUME AS PERFECTLY NORMAL MAY BE INSULTING TO OTHERS.

Giving the "thumbs up". You're trying to give someone praise with this sign of approval, but in Brazil, Greece, Turkey, Italy, Israel, Saudi Arabia, and Russia, you're actually saying, "Up yours!"

The "Two Up" Holding the middle finger and pointer finger is called the "two up" in much of Europe. This is an obscene gesture equivalent to the Western "middle finger".

Using the left hand. Some cultures have disdain for the left hand. Middle Eastern cultures use the left hand for any hygiene tasks below the waist, so using your left hand is considered unclean. Asians and Middle Easterners are insulted when you present something with your left hand.

Get a Leg Up on the Situation

What are your legs and feet saying to someone from a different culture? You might be surprised to find out that you just overstepped a cultural boundary.

Crossing legs. You've already learned that crossing your legs is considered a closed or defensive posture. But when you do this in the presence of certain people, you could be sending out an even worse signal. Many Middle Eastern cultures are insulted when you show the soles of your shoes, because they see that as the lowest part of your body, literally and figuratively.

Sitting with the "Figure 4" leg cross—one ankle resting on the opposite knee—is considered rude by Russians.

Removing shoes. You've probably seen this custom in the movies. It's a sign of respect to take off your shoes when entering the home of someone from Japan, Korea, the Philippines, or Thailand.

IF YOUR HOST IS SHOELESS OR REMOVES HIS SHOES, BE SURE TO DO THE SAME.

Spaced Out

You know about the four zones of space between people in Chapter 5—public, social, personal, and intimate. How does this translate into other cultures?

Closing in. Latin Americans and Greeks are close talkers. Some French and French Canadians will move closer as well.

Standing back. Asians and Indians prefer more distance between them and the people they're talking to, so don't be surprised if they are farther than the two-foot, conversational standard.

Hugging. Some cultures are more demonstrative, like Middle Easterners, Greeks, Italians, and Latin Americans, who are much more free with their hugs. Asians are not receptive to this type of close contact.

Touching. We value our personal space, but we sometimes overlook that our boundaries aren't universal. Touching other people, like Middle Eastern women and East Indian children is a definite no-no!

It's Not All Greek to Me

Communication has cultural boundaries. Just like you need to learn the vocabulary, grammar, and idioms of a foreign country to converse with people from there, you must take the time to understand the non-verbal aspect of their culture. With the global nature of doing business today, be sure that what your body is saying aligns with your words!

Your New Skills Set

We've discussed body language from head to toe and even taken it around the world. Eyes, mouth, arms, hands, legs, feet and distance—it all has meaning, and when you understand it, YOU become the mind reader. Remember, having this new skill set is powerful. It becomes your secret weapon when you not only watch the body language of others, but when you practice the skills yourself in the real world.

So be aware of your handshakes, the way you move your eyes, arms, and legs. You now have a real world, unfair advantage. You are armed and dangerous.

Since I'm ¼ Irish, I'll end with an Irish Blessing.

May the road rise up to meet you,

May the wind be always at your back,

May the sun shine warm upon your face,

The rain fall soft upon your fields,

And until we meet again,

May God hold you in the palm of His hand.